JESUS
CHANGES
EVERYTHING

BOB GEORGE

HARVEST HOUSE PUBLISHERS
EUGENE, OREGON

Cover by Koechel Peterson & Associates, Inc., Minneapolis, Minnesota

All personal examples in this book are true. Where individuals may be identifiable, they have granted the author and the publisher the right to use their names, stories, and/or facts of their lives in all manners, including composite or altered representations. In all other cases, names, circumstances, descriptions, and details have been changed to render individuals unidentifiable.

JESUS CHANGES EVERYTHING
Copyright © 2013 by Bob George
Published by Harvest House Publishers
Eugene, Oregon 97402
www.harvesthousepublishers.com

Library of Congress Cataloging-in-Publication Data

George, Bob, 1933-
Jesus changes everything / by Bob George.
    p. cm.
ISBN 978-0-7369-4890-6 (pbk.)
ISBN 978-0-7369-4891-3 (eBook)
1. Grace (Theology) I. Title.
BT761.3.G455 2013
234—dc23
                                                            2012026073

13 14 15 16 17 18 19 20 21 / BP-JH / 10 9 8 7 6 5 4 3 2 1

To Bob Hawkins Jr. and the staff of Harvest House Publishers:

"I thank my God every time I remember you. In all my prayers for all of you, I always pray with joy because of your partnership in the gospel from the first day until now, being confident of this, that he who began a good work in you will carry it on to completion until the day of Christ Jesus" (Philippians 1:3-6).

I also thank God for my wife, Amy, my daughter, Debbie, and my son, Bob, who have stood by me through all the difficulties and joys of life.

Contents

Why Does Jesus Change Everything?

"Jesus changes everything." This could easily be considered just another shallow Christian cliché. But I mean it with complete seriousness, and to a level that's hard to express.

Christ first changed my life in 1969 when my wife, Amy, and I heard the gospel and put our faith in him. The impact on me was dramatic—one of those darkness-to-light conversions. Previously egotistical, money-driven, and selfish, I turned into a man with brand-new sensitivities and a drive to help others come to know the Jesus who had changed me.

I discovered over the next 40 years that my conversion was only the beginning of many experiences of the kind of changes Jesus makes. Countless times I've had my understanding and expectations overhauled as the Lord opened my eyes to new truth about him, about me, and about life.

You can say that Jesus is all about change. He said he came to "give his life as a ransom for many" (Matthew 20:28), "to seek and to save the lost" (Luke 19:10); he came so that those who believe in him "may have life, and have it to the full" (John 10:10). As we read further in the New Testament we discover that ultimately all of creation will be renewed as a result of his work and under his lordship.

He has changed everything in this world's sphere already. Over much of the globe, today's date is determined by an estimate of the day he was born. However, as familiar as that reckoning is, we will see that it is off by about 33 years.

Why do I say this? It is because the real dividing point of history is not the birth of Christ, but his death on the cross. His death simultaneously fulfilled the Old Covenant—God's agreement with the people of Israel, made at Mount Sinai—and inaugurated the New Covenant—the new agreement God established, and the one under which we live today. This is the change that makes all the difference in the history of the universe, and all the difference in your life and mine.

That's why I have written this book to explain the New Covenant. In it, you will find new understanding of what Christ has done and will do for you. You'll get a rich picture of the kind of changes Jesus can and will make in your life if you put your trust in him for your day-to-day existence.

This may be the first time you learn of the changes Christ makes. Or Jesus may already have changed your life to an extent. Either way, there is more to come—much more than you have ever dreamed!

It is my hope that you will discover the richness of Christ, and also the wealth that is yours because of this New Covenant he has brought into being.

May his changes in your life be a rich journey of discovery until he takes you to the fullness of eternal life in his presence.

1

The Big Picture

What's the Issue? Why Is It So Important?

You may not be sure what I mean by saying that I am a New Covenant man. Or maybe you have an inkling from what I wrote on the previous pages. Either way, if you'll stick with me through this book, I promise to share with you the best news ever given to the human race. The New Covenant encompasses everything God has planned for his children from eternity past. It represents all he has done and will do for us through his Son, Jesus Christ. Those who understand and receive this good news find their lives permanently and dramatically transformed, and discover in it new hope, freedom, and power.

I have said for many years that if I have only one message to share before I die, it would be the message of the New Covenant. Before I complete my service on earth for Christ, there is one book I have wanted to write. It is this one. After reading it, I hope that you too will call yourself a New Covenant man or New Covenant woman. I hope that many young believers who are now children or teenagers will be taught this truth at the beginning of their Christian lives, so that they will have the knowledge and equipment to live wonderfully fruitful and joy-filled lives for our Savior and Lord.

It's obvious that many believers do not live "wonderfully fruitful and joy-filled lives." From my unique perspective of doing on-air counseling for over 25 years on the *People to People* radio program, I have had the opportunity to listen to thousands of callers express their confusion, frustration, and struggles about the Christian life. What I've observed is this: Today's Christians are among the most confused people on earth.

Bewildered by Contradictory Voices

Why do I say that today's Christians are confused? Here's a small sample of the kinds of questions I have been asked countless times by radio listeners.

"I went to one church," Josh said, "and the preacher said it was wrong to play sports on the Sabbath. I'm a member of a recreation-league basketball team, and we normally play on Sundays. I don't want to break the Ten Commandments. What am I supposed to do?"

An older woman named Charlotte called the program: "Our minister quoted the Bible and said that if we don't 'tithe to the storehouse' we are robbing God. He said if we don't tithe, God will take our money some other way. He told a scary story about a man in his previous church who wouldn't tithe, and then his house burned down!"

Matt called and read 2 Chronicles 7:14: "If my people, who are called by my name, will humble themselves and pray and seek my face and turn from their wicked ways, then I will hear from heaven, and I will forgive their sin and will heal their land." He said, "A speaker on a radio program quoted this verse and said that this is America's problem. He said there are groups trying to get rid of 'In God We Trust' on our money just like they got rid of prayer in the classroom. He wants Christians to sign petitions and call the White House and their congressmen to demand that we keep God in America. Then he said God will forgive us and send prosperity again."

Notice that a common theme runs through all of these questions. It is this: Live right and do the right things, God blesses. Fail, God punishes. This is what most people really think about God, and as a result they live in fear of his punishment. No wonder it's so difficult for so many Christians to truly believe they are loved by God. This mindset ultimately leads to uncertainty about God's acceptance and forgiveness and undermines our assurance that we've been born again. This was the case for Katie.

The Human Cost of Confusion

"Bob," Katie began, almost in tears, "I'm so confused and afraid. I feel like I'm walking on eggshells, just waiting for God to strike me down because of all the sins I've committed."

A close relative had filled her mind with a host of things she needed to do to be a "good" Christian. Katie had sincerely tried to live up to those standards, but had become frustrated and disillusioned. Before she had come to Christ, the message she received was "salvation is a free gift from God for those who believe." That is correct. That is the gospel. But the life she was now attempting to live hardly seemed like a gift. Trying to live the "perfect" Christian life was a burden, leaving her wondering whether or not she was even saved in the first place.

When believers are taught to look to themselves and their own works, the results can only be self-condemnation, guilt, insecurity, and fear. That's the kind of burden others were placing on Katie.

How can anyone think God wants his children to live like this? The answer, of course, is that he doesn't. The Scriptures overflow with God's desire that his children learn about and bask in the glory of his love and grace through Jesus Christ. Listen to what the apostle Paul wrote to the believers in Colossae:

> I want you to know how hard I am contending for you and for those at Laodicea, and for all who have not met me personally. My goal is *that they may be encouraged in heart and united in love, so that they may have the full riches of complete understanding,* in order that *they may know the mystery of God, namely, Christ,* in whom are hidden all the treasures of wisdom and knowledge (Colossians 2:1-3).

Does that sound like Paul wants believers to wallow in guilt and insecurity? A few verses later, he says,

> Just as you received Christ Jesus as Lord, continue to live your lives in him, *rooted and built up in him, strengthened in the faith* as you were taught, and *overflowing with* thankfulness (Colossians 2:6-7).

People like Katie have had their faith and understanding shaken by unsound teaching, and they experience the exact opposite of these verses. Instead of being "strengthened in her faith," Katie became insecure. Instead of "overflowing with gratitude," she wept from fear. Paul's images of being "rooted and built up in him" speak of strength, security, and nourishment. None of those descriptions characterized her.

What Katie needed was a shift in focus. In listening to her well-intentioned relative, she turned her eyes away from Jesus and onto herself. She came to think it was up to her to live the perfect Christian life. She had received a free gift, but now it was up to her to merit keeping it. And nothing can be further from the truth.

Finding a Life of Confidence

Katie had been taken hostage by what I call an Old Covenant mindset. Here is what I mean. A person living with an Old Covenant mindset is one who relies on rules and regulations as the means for gaining God's love and acceptance. Basically, this person's ability to carry out the rules and regulations defines his relationship with God. That is where the problem lies. We certainly cannot live up to the Ten Commandments. Even rules established by a church, or our own personal standards, condemn us.

With this mindset, you can't help but question God's love for you and your salvation. That is not what he intends for his children. He wants us to know and to live in the truth that we are eternally saved.

Concerning eternal security, the Bible is clear. Writing to believers being disturbed by cultlike teachings near the end of the first century, the apostle John expressed his overall purpose:

> This is the testimony: *God has given us eternal life, and this life is in his Son.* Whoever has the Son has life; whoever does not have the Son of God does not have life. I write

these things to you who believe in the name of the Son of
God *so that you may **know** that you have eternal life* (1 John
5:11-13).

There are people who deny the possibility of having absolute assurance of salvation. I always point them to 1 John 5:13. "John says I can
know that I have eternal life. You say I can't know. So I ask you: Who
should I believe? You or the Bible?"

My faith cannot be shaken, but it's not just because I know Bible
verses like this one. It's because I have come to know the much larger
truth that stands over all of it: the New Covenant. The failure to understand the New Covenant is the bigger issue behind the examples of
confusion I've shared. Understanding the New Covenant clears everything up and makes many of today's controversies moot.

For Katie, coming to understand her position under the New Covenant cleared up her confusion and enabled her to begin experiencing
the benefits Paul talked about: She became "rooted and grounded in
love" and "overflowing with thanksgiving." As we begin our explora-
tion, I have the same hope for you.

Introducing the New Covenant

So far I've shared several stories about the results of people's failure
to understand the New Covenant, but I haven't explained what it is.
The subject is so rich and comprehensive that I'll take the rest of this
book to spell it out, but let's get started.

The New Covenant is not "new" in the sense of recent. It is not
some novel angle on the Scripture that I thought up—nor do I claim
to be the recipient of some previously unknown special revelation. God
hinted at the New Covenant even in the Garden of Eden after our
first parents, Adam and Eve, fell into sin. It was promised to Abraham
more than 2100 years before Christ. Moses, in the 1400s BC, told of
a prophet greater than he was who would come one day (later identi-
fied as Jesus Christ) and prophesied of the New Covenant God would
make with his people. Then God began to speak specifically through

the prophets about this New Covenant that he would create in the future, sharing more of its details. You'll find it spelled out in the writings of Isaiah, Jeremiah, and Ezekiel, among others.

Hundreds of years of predictions preceded the night Jesus met with his disciples to celebrate the Passover, the traditional celebration of Israel's release from their bondage in Egypt. Knowing he would go to his death on the cross the following day, Jesus invested the observance with new significance:

> He took bread, gave thanks and broke it, and gave it to them, saying, "This is my body given for you; do this in remembrance of me" (Luke 22:19).

Jesus' words about his body given for us pointed to what his death would accomplish: the satisfaction of God's justice, the forgiveness of humanity's sins, the reconciliation of the world to God, and much more.

Most Christians grasp this, at least generally. Even many non-Christians, though unbelieving, understand that the purpose of Christ's death on the cross was to make man acceptable to God.

The significance of what Jesus said next, however, seems to have been missed for the most part:

> In the same way, after the supper he took the cup, saying, "This cup is the new covenant in my blood, which is poured out for you" (Luke 22:20).

Something Changed

Whatever the meaning of the term "the new covenant," it should be immediately clear from Jesus' words that something is about to change. If this is a "new" covenant, common sense would lead us to assume there must have been an "old" covenant. And there was. It is also known as the Law of Moses.

The apostle Paul was clearly aware of the difference. In describing his ministry to the Corinthians he says,

Such confidence we have through Christ before God. Not that we are competent in ourselves to claim anything for ourselves, but our competence comes from God. *He has made us competent as ministers of a new covenant*—not of the letter but of the Spirit; for the letter kills, but the Spirit gives life (2 Corinthians 3:4-6).

Paul boldly states that he is a servant of the New Covenant and sharply distinguishes it from the Old Covenant, which he calls "the letter." The effect of the old is to "kill," he says, but the new "gives life." It's hard to imagine effects further apart than death and life!

So there is no doubt that Jesus intended to signal the inauguration of the New Covenant, or that Paul clearly taught about that covenant. But there is another vitally important implication of Jesus' words during that Passover meal. Look again at the verse:

In the same way, after the supper he took the cup, saying, "This cup is the new covenant *in my blood, which is poured out for you*" (Luke 22:20).

Not only was Jesus announcing the beginning of the New Covenant, but he was also clearly pointing to the *time* of its inauguration. The New Covenant began at the *death* of Christ, not at his birth! It is the cross that is the center of history as far as God is concerned. We'll unfold the implications of this truth as we go on.

The New Covenant has huge ramifications for our understanding of the Bible and for Christian living. This understanding provides the key to free people from confusion and all those apparent "contradictions" in the Bible that we saw earlier in this chapter.

Jesus' Death and the New Covenant

The word *covenant* itself may be somewhat strange to you. For thousands of years in the ancient world, people were thoroughly familiar with covenants because they were an ordinary part of their lives. Not so in our day. I will go into a fuller explanation of what covenants were all about in chapter 4, but for now, the simplest modern comparison is what we call a "last will and testament." A testament and a covenant are the same thing, so we actually could speak of a person's "last will and covenant."

The purpose of a will is to allow someone to decide in advance how his assets will be distributed following his death. I have a will, for example, that spells out how my property will be left to my wife, Amy, to my two children and their families, and to the People to People ministry. If you are an adult, I certainly hope you have made a will.

How does this relate to our discussion? In the ancient world they also had wills, and the writer of Hebrews uses that everyday reality to make an important point about the death of Christ as it relates to the New Covenant:

> In the case of a will, it is necessary to prove the death of the one who made it, because a will is in force only when somebody has died; it never takes effect while the one who made it is living (Hebrews 9:16-17).

Let's suppose that I own a vintage sports car, and in my will I have decided to leave it to you. Let's also suppose that you've found a copy of my will, read it, and are delighted to discover that you would inherit that sports car. So, with my last will and testament in hand, you come to the house and ask for the keys. "See?" you say. "It's written right here."

Sorry, it doesn't work that way. No matter what is written in a person's will, it does not take effect until the person who made it dies, just as the writer of Hebrews says above.

The New Covenant Put into Effect

The writer of Hebrews also points out that even the Old Covenant, the Law of Moses, had to be put into effect by a death—in this case, through the symbolic substitutionary death involving blood sacrifices:

> This is why even the first covenant was not put into effect without blood. When Moses had proclaimed every command of the law to all the people, he took the blood of calves,

together with water, scarlet wool and branches of hyssop, and sprinkled the scroll and all the people. He said, "This is the blood of the covenant, which God has commanded you to keep" (Hebrews 9:18-20).

The principle illustrated is that *only death puts a covenant into effect.* Therefore the writer concludes,

In fact, the law requires that nearly everything be cleansed with blood, and without the shedding of blood there is no forgiveness (Hebrews 9:22).

Take careful note of that last line, a critically important spiritual principle: *"Without the shedding of blood there is no forgiveness."* The Bible, from beginning to end, describes the character of God as being merciful, compassionate, forgiving, and full of grace—*and at the same time, and in the same measure*—holy, righteous, just, and uncompromising with evil. "The great problem of the Bible," if I may use that phrase, is this: *How can God forgive guilty, sinful, evil human beings while at the same time expressing his holy, righteous, and just nature?* The answer is hinted at in the Old Testament: *Only through the death of an innocent substitute.* The animal sacrifices demanded under the Law of Moses were illustrations of this truth. But they could never truly deal with the sin problem, as we will see. Only an infinitely perfect sacrifice could redeem the human race, and that is exactly what Jesus Christ came to do. Only his death on the cross could be a sufficient sacrifice.

We will explore this wonderful truth in detail in the chapters ahead. For now, consider how the death of Christ affects our discussion of a covenant. A last will and testament is only put into effect by the death of the one who made it. Recall the words of Jesus we looked at earlier, words he spoke the night before his death:

In the same way, after the supper he took the cup, saying, *"This cup is the new covenant in my blood*, which is poured out for you" (Luke 22:20).

Do you hear what he is saying? As with a Last Will and Testament,

Jesus is indicating that his death the next day would put into effect the long-promised, long-awaited New Covenant.

We Are Heirs

What does this mean to you and me? We need to understand what this New Covenant is, and what it entails. How can we know that we are heirs of this promise? How can we be sure we are in on it? One thing we can know right up front: Participation in it comes through a relationship with the one who made it, Jesus Christ.

Therefore, the first question to consider is whether you have received Christ. Are you rightly related to him?

> To all who did receive him, to those who believed in his name, he gave the right to become children of God (John 1:12).

Have you "believed in his name"? Have you recognized that the one and only way you could ever be reconciled to a holy God is through the mediation of a Savior, the Son of God, who voluntarily went to death on a cross in your place? If so, you can boldly and joyfully proclaim that you are a child of God.

There is much more good news besides. Paul writes,

> If we are children, *then we are heirs*—heirs of God and co-heirs with Christ, if indeed we share in his sufferings in order that we may also share in his glory (Romans 8:17).

By saying "share in his sufferings," Paul means facing the particular types of trouble you can receive by being a Christian in a world in rebellion against God. That's certainly true, and the Bible never sugar-coats that possibility. But more important to who we are: We are "heirs of God"! Have you ever considered that and what it might mean?

What if a stranger appeared at your door one day to notify you that a "rich uncle" you'd never heard of had just died and you were named the principal heir in his will. Don't you think you'd hurry to find out more information? Of course! Well, according to God's Word, if you are a Christian, you are a "principal heir" in *God's* will.

That means that if you are "in Christ," as an heir of the New Covenant...

- you are totally forgiven for your sins.
- you stand before God as righteous in his sight as Jesus Christ himself.
- you have been bought, or redeemed, by Christ, meaning you are God's beloved possession.
- you have received the very life of the resurrected Christ through the Holy Spirit, who has come to indwell you forever.
- you have been given a "new heart"; you have been raised to life in Christ with a new nature like his.
- you possess eternal life, which can never be lost or taken away.
- you can have total assurance of salvation, knowing beyond the shadow of a doubt that you have eternal life.
- you can have boldness and confidence to enter the presence of God.
- you have been introduced into a life of "Sabbath rest," no longer working to earn or maintain your relationship with God, but trusting that Christ has done it once and for all.
- you will find that the Bible really does make sense, and you'll grow in your confidence to read and interpret it for yourself.

The New Covenant Is the Key

If you are wondering if these things are a possibility for you, let me share a story with you about my friend Evelyn. Evelyn attends our local fellowship in Carrollton, Texas. One day during our midweek Bible study she told us about her journey into the New Covenant:

> A few years back, things were a mess in my life, and I so desperately wanted the peace of God. I came from a family where my parents taught us to go to church, and life was good. So I decided to spend more time and participate at the church to fill the void. This, I thought, would bring me closer to God.
>
> I began to attend church regularly. Then I included the midweek studies and joined the women's group. I soon found myself president of that women's group, and I was at the church every time the doors were open. It was a busy time…planning and carrying out fund-raising events, visiting the sick and elderly, and meeting with church officials. I was always at the church—so much so that the pastor gave me my own *key to the church*. I thought I had arrived. But when I really took stock of my life, I still did not have peace in my heart. In my pursuit of the peace of God in my life, my efforts became a chore, and the void was still there.
>
> It was during this time a dear friend of mine shared with me the message of grace and the New Covenant, and she invited me to attend her church. It was like my heart smiled—I was drawn to that teaching because I needed to know the love of God that would fill the void in my life. I needed to know what God had already done for me and not what I could do for Him. I'm so grateful to those at People to People Ministries, who continually teach that New Covenant message. And now being a part of that church body, I see their lives are lived the same way…in dependence on the grace of God…Christ Jesus.
>
> Looking back, I know that those things occurred as part of my journey to be where I am today…anchored in the love of Christ. Not needing a key to the church, because I *am* part of the church; but now possessing the *key to the kingdom*… the peace of God.

Evelyn discovered that Christ's finished work on the cross closed the door on her old, burdened life of fear, guilt, and failure and set her free to draw near to Jesus and share his resurrected life. The New Covenant was the key. That key is available to you as well.

In my early years as a Christian, I heard very little about the New Covenant. It is a subject seldom preached from the pulpit. As a matter of fact, in all of my years of being in church, I don't recall ever hearing a sermon on this topic. Why the church has neglected the most important and dynamic message explaining our relationship with Jesus Christ is beyond me. In my opinion, the great news of the New Covenant needs to be shouted from the rooftops.

I unabashedly claim to be a New Covenant man. There is no other message worth proclaiming. Learning to rest in Jesus Christ and all that he accomplished changed my life. I want that for you as well.

2

The Legalistic Paradox

Why Christians Hide What's Inside

I began this book by proclaiming that I am a New Covenant man. How I became a New Covenant man is a longer story.

In my previous three books I have explained in detail how I became a Christian when I was 36 years old, entered the ministry shortly after, and went on to found my own ministry before a decade had passed. I won't tell the entire story again, but I must emphasize the second turning point when my life changed. It certainly changed in many true and wonderful ways when I received Christ as my Savior, but there was much, much more to learn. I hit a "spiritual ceiling," against which I battered my head until the Lord got me through by teaching me about the New Covenant. I'm so thankful to say he did. In a way, I was "born again *again*."

There was no problem with my sincerity or work ethic as a Christian. I was busy speaking at conferences, leading a discipleship and church-consulting ministry, writing Bible study materials, and doing a daily radio broadcast. I led several groups a week—Bible studies in homes, leadership breakfasts, and staff training. Always on the bold side (my business background was as a salesman), I loved personal evangelism, and I had the opportunity to personally lead *hundreds* of individuals to faith in Christ.

What could be wrong? Simple. I was busy, all right, but inwardly I had become barren. I was dried up inside, which only made me redouble my efforts to serve the Lord. Finally, I reached a crisis one morning while driving down a Dallas freeway to our office. With tears streaming down my cheeks, I loudly sang a song recorded about that time by Andraé Crouch: *Lord, take me back to the days I first knew you…*

I wasn't just singing a song. My heart was crying out a prayer to my heavenly Father, asking what was wrong with me. If there's anything that should characterize the Christian life, according to the New Testament, it is the quality of *joy*. I had once had it. I remembered how, after I had received Christ into my life, I overflowed with it. It was the reason sharing the gospel with others became so much more interesting, motivating, and fulfilling than any amount of money I was making in my floor-covering business. Joy was the reason I originally joined the full-time ministry a couple of years later, and why I worked so hard leading evangelistic campaigns and discipleship programs. But somewhere along the way, I had lost it. In my heart I was begging God to tell me where I had gone wrong and how to find my way back.

One of the worst aspects of that period of my life was that even while I was weeping and crying out to God inside, *no one knew it*. I still had a strong dose of what I call "fleshly pride" in my ministry efforts. It's easy to do when you have natural strengths that can be called upon to do "spiritual work."

But the Lord has very creative and often surprising ways of exposing the reality of our lives! He doesn't let hypocrites get away with their hypocrisy for long.

Pride Reveals the Heart

It was the fall of 1978. The ministry I had founded less than two years before was staffed by many sincere but inexperienced people. I was feeling pretty full of myself, and I worked up an indignant attitude about my staff. They just weren't bold enough about witnessing! I decided to do something about it.

I remember telling the vice-president of our ministry, Don Ostroff,

"Our staff needs to develop some boldness. They're too passive. How can we teach church people about witnessing if our own staff is too scared to do it?" Like me, Don had come out of another organization in which we did a lot of evangelistic witnessing to strangers on beaches, street corners, and other public places. We were very proud of our "boldness for Christ."

I don't think Don was too excited, but he agreed to go along with the plan. So I announced to our staff that we were loading up some vans and were going witnessing door-to-door. Every one of them had the "deer in the headlights" look, and there were some big gulps, but nobody refused. Off we went.

We drove to Lakewood, a very beautiful part of Dallas with long tree-lined streets and very large homes. Teaming up two by two, I took my colleague Tim Stevenson, and we started down one side of the street. Tim was still a new Christian. He had some teaching potential, I thought, but was not much for witnessing. I was absolutely sure I could impress him with my boldness and great techniques in sharing the gospel with strangers.

We walked up to one really large home and rang the bell. A woman who appeared to be dressed as a maid opened the door. "We're visiting from ——— church," I began, "and we'd like to talk to someone here about Jesus Christ and eternal life." I was really smooth and confident. I was sure Tim was impressed.

"There's nobody home," the woman answered, "except me."

"Well, that's okay," I said. "May I take a few minutes to share with you how you can have a full and wonderful life?"

The woman shrugged. "I guess so," she said.

I opened the little witnessing booklet in my hand and began my well-practiced presentation. Reading the first line, I said, "People want to have a life that is full and meaningful. How about you?" I paused. "By the way, what is your name?" (If you're a trained salesman, you know you always want to use your prospect's name frequently in your sales pitch.)

"Djgjn," she mumbled. At least it sounded that way.

"Pardon me?" I leaned in. "What is your name?"

"Dddgjjn," she mumbled. Out of the corner of my eye, I could see Tim wore a puzzled look. He evidently didn't understand her, either.

"It sounded like you said…'Dragon'?" I said in a questioning tone.

She nodded. Tim's eyes got wider and he stood very still. I had never heard of anyone named "Dragon" before, but there's a first time for everything.

I launched right in with my booklet, intent on demonstrating excellence and boldness in evangelism and using my salesmanship skills. Pointing to the illustrations, I asked, "Now, Dragon, which of these diagrams represents your life?" She cooperatively answered each of my questions.

I walked her page by page through the booklet.

"Now, Dragon, people often try to earn God's acceptance through many ways…"

"Think about it this way, Dragon, if God is perfect, how good would you have to be to earn your way to heaven?"…

"For God so loved the world…and that's *you*, Dragon…that he gave…"

For 25 minutes it went that way. I finally got to the big finish, the prayer to receive salvation. "Now, Dragon, would you like to pray right now and ask Jesus Christ to come into your life?"

She suddenly almost shouted, "*My name's not 'Dragon'!*"

Obviously, this witnessing encounter was in shambles. On the positive side, *Jernigan* claimed that she actually already was a Christian.

It's probably needless to say, but it was the last time I made the staff go out witnessing to strangers.

Yes, it's funny now, but at the time it was a very troubling discovery. In my zeal to get my staff to become bold witnesses, I had crossed over a line of self-deception. While appearing to be dedicated to evangelism, I was more concerned with techniques and being a "good example." In my heart, I didn't want to be fake. I wanted reality. But how?

The Legalistic Paradox

I started off this chapter by telling you about the misery and heart-break I was experiencing during this time of my life. And now I've just shared a story *that happened during that same period*—a story where I exhibited pride, arrogance, and self-dependence. At the same time I was driving to work with tears streaming down my cheeks singing, *Lord, take me back to the days I first knew you,* I was strutting around showing off my "boldness for Christ."

Those qualities might appear at first glance to be exact opposites, but I have learned they are not. In fact, they are predictable characteristics of people who sincerely try to live "religious" lives apart from New Covenant truth.

This is the "legalistic paradox": The same human efforts that utterly fail to gain the approval of God or produce his quality of life can turn around and become the ground of human competition, pride, arrogance, and judgmental attitudes. Then, because of their inability to live up to what they claim they experience, people have to don "masks" and become pretenders. It is religion, not New Covenant reality, that leads to hypocrisy.

Living by Law

From the first sentence of this book I have spoken of being a "New Covenant man." But I have not yet explained what the alternative might be. What would you call a Christian who is something other than a New Covenant man or woman?

There are many possible choices. How about an "Old Covenant man"? That doesn't work, because no one, not even the Jewish people of today, truly attempt to live according to the whole Law of Moses. It's not even possible, because since AD 70 there have been no priesthood, no Temple, and no sacrifices. (Judaism was redefined and restructured by the rabbis around AD 200. It was turned into a religion that could be practiced by the Jewish people in the form of tradition without the Old Covenant essentials as they dispersed all over the globe.)

How about a "religious Christian"? In some ways, that works. I have always liked the statement, "Christianity isn't a religion. It is a *relationship* with God through his Son, Jesus Christ." "Religion" in this context refers to *man's efforts to reach up to God to earn acceptance.*

The gospel is about *God's work to reach down to man in forgiveness and acceptance through Jesus Christ.* So contrasting "religion" with being a New Covenant man works to some extent. But for many people, it's still too vague.

Perhaps for now, the best designation is that of a "legalistic Christian." I will have to explain what I mean by "legalism," and I will as we move ahead. Another way of saying the same thing is to refer to a Christian who is "living by law." That again requires explanation because, as mentioned above, no one really attempts to live according to all the Law of Moses. After we explore this some more in the remainder of this book, I believe you will understand it clearly.

The "Law Principle"

First, an important clarification: The word *law* has different meanings depending on what you intend to convey. *Law* as a *covenant* refers specifically to the Law of Moses, or the Old Covenant. When I am using this meaning, I will capitalize the word. *Law* in this sense means the whole system of God's commandments that are spelled out in the Old Testament books of Exodus, Leviticus, Numbers, and Deuteronomy. A person then trying to "live by the Law" would be doing so with full intention, awareness, and conviction.

On the other hand, *law* as a *principle* can refer to any system of works, whether God-given or man-made, by which a person attempts to approach God. In this sense, you are "living by law" if you are trying to earn God's acceptance by your good actions, by the style, fervency, or length of your worship, through the way you serve others, or by the moral quality of your life. Someone "living by law" in this sense often is unconscious of it.

"Living by law" in this way comes as naturally as breathing to human beings. It comes from the natural religious impulses of human nature, and we don't know any better until it is corrected through coming to know the gospel of Jesus Christ. Only discovering New Covenant truth sets people completely free of it.

For those who are unfamiliar with this idea of living under law as a principle, it's often hard to grasp. It can be as large as the whole

Christian culture we live in, so we don't even notice it. An old Chinese proverb says, "If you want to know what water is, don't ask the fish." We tend to accept without question the same assumptions and opinions as the people we identify with.

These legalisms tend to change over time, and be different in different places. We often look with amusement at the laws and rules of past generations while failing to be aware of our own. In the early twentieth century, for example, it was simply assumed that "Christians don't drink, smoke, or chew, or run around with girls who do." Some church leaders were adamant in their opposition to dancing of any kind, to playing card games, and to businesses being open on Sunday, teaching that it was a violation of the Sabbath commandment.

Once, after Amy and I were converted, we attended a retreat for married couples at a camp. We couples were enjoying the pool, when the camp director ran up to us throwing a fit and demanding that we all leave. It turned out that this camp had a policy against "mixed bathing," as it was called. "Do you mean," I asked, "that I can sleep with my wife at this camp, but I can't *swim* with her?" Right, I was told.

Yes, those examples sound like something from a day gone by, but don't be too quick to laugh. Legalism morphs like Jell-O with each new generation. Today you'll hear a whole new list of things "good Christians" do or don't do. Good Christians feed starving children, they dig water wells in third-world countries, they do service in poor areas, and they support a "green planet." What's wrong with those things? Nothing at all—*except* when they become plumb lines by which we measure our or other people's spirituality, and become the basis of judging others. Other examples of modern "laws" (which often come in the form of unspoken expectations) have to do with how you are supposed to behave and feel during "worship"—a word I put in quotation marks, because today's ideas of worship do not necessarily reflect the biblical meaning of the word.

It's not about bad things. In fact, the seductive thing about law as a principle is that the rules, laws, or expectations are typically things that are good in and of themselves. You can make a good, logical case that it's wise to abstain from alcohol and tobacco. You can make an easy case that Christians ought to do good works in the world. *What is wrong, however, is when these practices subtly become the way we earn or maintain the acceptance of God.* That's when they become "laws."

The most important thing to grasp about the distinction between living by the Law and living by law as a principle is this: Though it's critically important to maintain for clear communication, *the distinction makes no difference in application.* The *effects* of trying to live up to the God-given Law or to man-made laws are exactly the same!

Characteristics of Someone Living by Law

Let's look at the characteristics of someone who is "living by law," thus being led by the law outwardly (see Romans 2:28-29). If legalistic living comes naturally to us simply because of our human natures, how would we know? What could serve as warning signs that you or I may be missing out on experiencing everything the Lord wants to give us through the New Covenant?

Avoiding God

God has made people for a relationship. It is part of our unique creation "in the image of God" (Genesis 1:27). While the animal kingdom can be functionally pleasing to God, no animal can know him personally. We, however, have been created with the capacity to know him and walk with him in a personal relationship. This truth is consistent from the beginning to the end of the Bible.

It was taught in the Old Testament:

> He has shown you, O mortal, what is good. And what does the Lord require of you? To act justly and to love mercy *and to walk humbly with your God* (Micah 6:8).

It was taught by the Lord Jesus Christ. In defining eternal life, he said,

> This is eternal life: that *they know you,* the only true God, *and Jesus Christ,* whom you have sent (John 17:3).

The apostles also emphasized the central importance of our relationship with God our Father, and with our Lord Jesus Christ. Paul wrote,

> What is more, I consider everything a loss because of the surpassing worth of *knowing Christ Jesus* my Lord...I want to *know Christ*... (Philippians 3:8,10).

The first predictable characteristic of legalism is that we will avoid dealing with God in a personal way. Oh, we'll continue going through the motions. We'll say prayers, go to church, continue doing religious activities. We'll still cry out to him in our times of need. But open our hearts to really *listen* to him? No. It's too threatening.

Apart from New Covenant truth, we will tend to trust in ourselves, in our efforts, and in our works to be "good enough" for God. And in truth, we will *never* be "good enough." So what can we do but deny that uncomfortable knowledge and sweep it under the rug of our lives? How much easier it is to emphasize our actions! How much more comfortable it is to be "religious"! But deal with God person to Person? No, that's too uncomfortable. This is the consequence that leads to all the others.

Guilt and Shame

The Bible clearly says throughout what is summarized in Romans 3:23: "All have sinned and fall short of the glory of God." Therefore, all human beings must deal in one way or another with the problem of guilt and shame.

Guilt and shame are not necessarily the same thing. Moral guilt is an objective truth: We have fallen short in our nature, character, and performance as measured against God's holiness. It is true whether or not we are aware of it, and whether or not we feel what we call guilt feelings.

Shame, on the other hand, is our experience of feelings of guilt, and may or may not be valid measured against God's truth. The old saying "Let your conscience be your guide" is helpful only insofar as our conscience is formed by the Scriptures. But the problem with the human conscience is that it can be trained in a number of ways, and not necessarily true ones. Members of organized crime groups can feel "guilty" for failing to support the criminal activities of the group. Dedicated members of the Nazi party would have felt "shame" for failing to turn in Jewish neighbors. Those are extreme examples, I know, but they show how the human conscience can be warped and perverted.

In my years on the *People to People* call-in program, I have talked with countless people who feel shame for doing things God never condemned. If you think back to our earlier discussion of legalism and law as a principle, you can imagine how many Christians have felt shame before God for drinking a beer or going to a dance, or for buying something on Sunday, believing they were breaking the Sabbath. God didn't create any of those laws and rules, but people felt guilty nonetheless.

In very sad cases, even victims of child abuse or sexual abuse often feel personal "shame" and "guilt"—they are unable to shake the belief that they were somehow "at fault" for what happened to them.

If you are wrestling with feelings like I've described, I have very good news for you. Christ told us the answer: "If you abide in my word...*you will know the truth, and the truth will set you free*" (John 8:31-32 ESV)!

If there's anything clearly observable about human beings, it's that we cannot live with guilt. We must do something with it. We have to get rid of it somehow. That's why so much human activity has to do with blaming someone else ("My mother made me this way"), or with offering excuses and justifications for our actions ("It wasn't my fault; I couldn't help myself").

We know in our hearts that we are responsible for our choices, and so we must find some way to deal with that fact. While all of us try to off-load our guilt in one way or another, nothing truly works. *Only the gospel of Jesus Christ offers human beings a genuine and healthy way to deal with guilt.* Our instincts are right—only by *transferring* guilt can it be removed, as John the Baptist recognized:

> John saw Jesus coming toward him and said, "Look, the Lamb of God, who *takes away* the sin of the world!" (John 1:29).

Jesus' death on the cross is the only answer to man's guilt before God. Only there can man's sins be transferred from us, taken away from us, enabling us to be forgiven.

Almost all Christians understand this in a general sense. However, apart from clear New Covenant understanding, believers' understanding of their forgiveness will be deficient. They will continue to believe they must *do something* to be fully forgiven. Therefore they continue to have a sense of guilt, which drives them away from their confident relationship with God.

Fear

This point is probably self-evident. What can a person feel who believes he or she is guilty before God but *fear*? And this fear will be all the worse the more a person understands the character of God as taught in the Scriptures. *"Be holy because I, the LORD your God, am holy"* says the Lord (Leviticus 19:1-2—among many other similar commands in both testaments).

In everyday life, fear can have as its object God, a grizzly bear, the sound of a truck's horn as we are crossing the street, or a news report about a terrorist attack. We most commonly use *fear* today to refer to our reaction to danger.

It is important to clarify that this type of fear is different from the very positive quality called the "fear of God," a term used throughout the Bible. For example, in Proverbs 1:7, we are told, "The fear of the LORD is the beginning of knowledge." Throughout the Scriptures, the main meaning of "the fear of the Lord" is the desirable quality of "reverent faith, awe, and worship." This is something we should *want* to cultivate.

However, there is a "fear of God" believers are not to have: the craven, fearful attitude that God is your enemy, as if he is your opponent out to hurt you. But this must follow if we aren't clear on New Covenant truth. If we know that God is holy, this means we also understand he must judge all evil and sin. Apart from knowing with confidence the answer to our sin and guilt—the full forgiveness of Jesus Christ—we will flee from God. Of course we cannot literally escape his presence, but we'll try to do so in our minds.

I've met believers who admit they've been running from God for decades, fearful that because they've never been good enough, his judgment is right around the corner. Thankfully, through learning of the New Covenant, many of these people have found the peace and joy of resting in the Lord's total acceptance and their position before him.

Lack of Ability to Love God or People

When he was asked what the greatest of all the commandments in the Law was, Jesus said,

> "Love the Lord your God with all your heart and with all your soul and with all your mind and with all your strength." The second is this: "Love your neighbor as yourself." There is no commandment greater than these (Mark 12:30-31).

Many people who know little about the Bible know this. Many unbelievers know that Jesus also said,

> A new command I give you: Love one another. As I have loved you, so you must love one another. By this everyone will know that you are my disciples, if you love one another (John 13:34-35).

The Word of God could not be clearer. But we also know we would rather have our "spirituality" evaluated on any ground other than love. If only Jesus had said something else! If only he had said all men will know we are his disciples by...our bumper stickers...the jeweled crosses we wear...how much we help the poor and homeless...the church activities we do...our work for justice in the political arena... and so on, and so on. But no. He said love is the measure. That's why you see so much of what I call "showing off for Jesus." It means self-conscious public piety. It's when we're out there in the world posturing and speaking in ways the world frankly finds weird, but we deceive ourselves into believing we look spiritual. It fails miserably to impress non-Christians or to interest them in Jesus.

However, we all know, if we are being honest, that we fall terribly short of God's definition of love. Why? Most believers know they *should* love God and others. Most believers *want* to love God and others. Why don't we love more?

Once again, the answer is right there in the Scriptures:

> This is love: *not that we loved God, but that he loved us* and sent his Son as an atoning sacrifice for our sins... *We love because he first loved us* (1 John 4:10,19).

The Law of Moses commanded the Israelites to love the Lord and to love their neighbor as themselves. But the problem with the Law, as we'll see later, is that while it can clearly *command* people to do God's will, *it provides them no power to carry it out.*

Only in the New Covenant do we gain both the *motivation* and the *power* to love God and others. We will learn in chapters ahead how God has done this. For now, let it suffice to say that, unless believers are transformed by receiving the love of God the Father and the Lord Jesus Christ through the Holy Spirit, they will be unable to pass that love on to God or other people.

Pride and Judgmental Attitudes

Here's where the "legalistic paradox" shows up. Even though the characteristics of someone living under law include guilt, fear, and avoiding God, still the legalist can develop incredible pride in his own "righteousness," which naturally becomes the platform from which he can become unmercifully judgmental toward other "sinners."

Here's what happens. Because of the effects that come from living by law—guilt, fear, and avoiding God—the legalist will deal with those feelings by *redefining what it means to be a "good Christian" by inventing more reachable standards.* It's somewhat like a high jumper who looks at an impossible standard, say 18 feet, and realizes he'll never make it over the bar. So what does he do? He lowers the bar to 18 inches and declares that to be the standard of excellent high jumping. He steps right over it and feels a glow of achievement.

If you think that's on the absurd side, just look at the evangelical world around you. Listen to Christian radio and ask what they're communicating in answer to the question, "What is your definition of a 'good Christian'?" Chances are very high that they will be promoting anything *but* the qualities of love, mercy, and grace that our Lord and Savior has given us…anything but *being like Jesus.*

We have added all kinds of "unwritten commandments" in the Christian community. There are few things more exhausting or more demoralizing than trying to live up to the expectations of others, but countless believers try to do just that. Learning to walk like, talk like, and hold the opinions of our Christian circle becomes the dominant concern when we have lost sight of what the Bible actually teaches that God wants.

Instead of the old legalisms like drinking, smoking, and dancing, today's believers are more likely to judge others by the opinions they hold. Many have recognized and spoken against the cultural value of political correctness, but how many believers have recognized that many of us have our version of the same thing? I call it being "evangelically correct." In some groups it is unthinkable that a Christian could support a Republican candidate. In other places it is exactly the opposite, and "no sincere Christian could ever vote for a Democrat." Woe to the believer who admits out loud that he or she supports the "wrong" side! You might as well admit you have leprosy.

Man-made laws, rules, and expectations currently tend to be more in the areas of social action and good works than explicitly in doctrine. But the shunning of "unacceptable opinions" today is just as strong as the old rejection of anyone who drank alcohol or didn't go to church on Sunday.

And just like the legalisms of the past, any one of these standards can be chosen by an individual legalist to "prove" that he or she is a good Christian, and can then be used to condemn other believers who don't practice the "rule."

As I shared in the "Dragon" story, for me being a good Christian meant being a "bold witness." I looked down on other Christians who were afraid to talk to strangers about Jesus (which covers most normal people). I had all this proof, I thought, to demonstrate how "spiritual" I was. And it was all a façade.

Pride and judgmental attitudes will always be found where the New Covenant is not understood, taught, and practiced.

Lack of Peace, Rest, or Joy in One's Spiritual Life

You'll find in many Christians a restlessness, a continual search for "something more." Whatever it is that's missing, they hope it will be found through the next revival, the next worship music "high," the next retreat, the next recommitment, the next big effort for God. On and on they go, never experiencing what Jesus offered—*rest* (Matthew 11:28-30).

The New Testament especially overflows with joy. "Rejoice always," says Paul (1 Thessalonians 5:16). "Rejoice in the Lord always. I will say it again: Rejoice!" (Philippians 4:4). Joy is so characteristic as a fruit of the gospel of Jesus Christ that writer G.K. Chesterton called joy "the gigantic secret of the Christian."

But you won't find it where legalism reigns. You might find excitement, diversion, fun, stimulation—but joy? No. Joy is a fruit of the Spirit (Galatians 5:22), and only in the New Covenant do you find the full expression of the Holy Spirit's work in believers.

The person living under law, on the other hand, can never rest, will not stop to be thankful, and surely cannot rejoice in tribulations and trials. Only the New Covenant produces joy and peace that are independent of circumstances.

Prepared to Learn Afresh

As I said at the beginning of this chapter, I had once been energized, motivated, and driven by joy. Somewhere I had lost it. I asked God from the depths of my heart to lead me back.

There was nothing wrong with my doctrine. I had been an avid Bible student and had taken advanced seminary-level courses. If you had given me a test on biblical doctrine, I would have passed with high marks. But there's a big difference in knowing information in your head and knowing the truth in your heart. Somewhere between my head and my heart there was a disconnect.

I was also to find that many of the truths I knew in my head were subtly twisted or misconceived. What led me to this discovery? The Lord Jesus, I remembered, had said, "You will know the truth, and the truth will set you free" (John 8:31-32). I reasoned with myself, *If it's right to say that the truth will set you free, then what is it that puts a person in bondage? It can only be error, lies, or deception. I'm certainly not free! Therefore there must be some error or lies in my thinking.*

It's humbling when you're a Christian leader to admit you don't know answers that are so crucial, but I had become miserable enough to become humbly teachable. I began to tell the Lord from the depths of my heart that I was willing to start over, and I asked him to teach me afresh from square one. I'm so grateful to say all these years later that the Lord answered my prayers beyond my imagination!

What about you? I don't know if you are as confused or as miserable as I was as I tried to live a Christian life. Perhaps you feel you're doing well and want to learn more. Either way, we all have much more to learn, and my prayer for you is that you will be open to listening to what the Word of God has to say to you.

3

A Path to New Covenant Understanding
"Aha!" Moments from God's Word

The New Covenant is a very large truth. No one grasps it in a day. It is typically a step-by-step, connect-the-dots process, through which we get the whole picture. But each "aha!" moment of discovery is so great and sheds so much light on your understanding of the Bible that at the moment you *feel* that you "get the whole thing." Looking back at my own journey of discovery, there must have been half a dozen times where I gained an insight and reacted, "That's it! I see it now! I get it!"... only to discover there was more to learn.

I have also learned that there are many "entry points" to the trail and many ways to the summit. Back in the 1980s I became acquainted with the fine Bible teacher and author Bill Gillham (Bill went to be with the Lord in 2011). We had become aware of each other and of similarities in our teaching, so we decided to spend some time together comparing our views. We found that we had come to the same conclusions, but through different paths.

Bill had a characteristic way of explaining the New Covenant as being made up of two major parts, like two sides of the same coin. "Side A" for Bill meant *Christ in you*—how through the Holy Spirit Christ lives his life in and through us, imparting to us a new motivation and new power. "Side B" in his language referred to *you in Christ*— how our position in Christ is the basis of our acceptance and identity.

In the middle of a conversation where I was telling my story, Bill suddenly stopped me with an amazed expression. "You got Side B first!" he exclaimed. In other words, I had first learned the depth and meaning of being *in Christ* first, and later learned the meaning of *Christ living in me*. For Bill it had been the other way around, and for the next couple of days, he continued to remark on what was to him a surprising discovery.*

I have learned that different biblical truths open people's minds to New Covenant understanding. You can't tell in advance which one will turn on the lights. I've learned to approach teaching it as if I have a ring full of keys. I don't know which one will open the lock, but I'll keep trying different ones until I find one that works. So, as I share how God worked in my life, remember that there's no single "right way" to walk the path to New Covenant understanding. Take in the truths we'll look at in the chapters ahead, and allow God to do his work in your life as he pleases.

Forgiveness and Reconciliation

After I had begun to pray, "Lord, take me back," the first place he directed my attention was to the issue of forgiveness. To put it bluntly, what I had been taught wasn't working.

The issue of God's forgiveness is always front and center when the gospel is proclaimed. We say to the world, "Jesus Christ died on the cross to provide forgiveness of sins to whosoever believes in him. Put your faith in him and receive the gift of eternal life." That is certainly true. It's what we say *after* people become believers that becomes the problem.

I was pretty well taught on my entry into the faith, and I became an avid student of the Bible. One of the things that was emphasized to me as a new Christian was the "total forgiveness" of my sins, meaning sins "past, present, *and future*." This was emphasized because only through this assurance can someone know that he or she has eternal

---

* Bill Gillham passes on his insights into New Covenant living in the book *Lifetime Guarantee* (Harvest House, 2012).

life and can never lose it. One of the passages often quoted to support this doctrine of total security is this:

> When you were dead in your sins and in the uncircumcision of your flesh, God made you alive with Christ. *He forgave us all our sins*, having canceled the charge of our legal indebtedness, which stood against us and condemned us; he has taken it away, nailing it to the cross (Colossians 2:13-14).

Certainly, this is a wonderful promise! However, often in the same lecture or sermon I was hearing, the speaker would go on to exhort us to "keep short accounts with God." What did they mean by that? They taught that while we were "judicially" forgiven "past, present, and future," to keep our "fellowship" with God we had to *do* something to receive "experiential forgiveness."

Am I Forgiven or Not?

If I had honestly shared my reactions at the time, I would have said that this sounded like double-talk. *Am I forgiven or not?* was my inner question. There were no passages of Scripture where the apostles talked about some kind of distinction between two kinds of forgiveness. There were no passages where "keeping short accounts with God" was taught in the New Testament.

Later, when I had the chance to read through the Bible on my own, I looked in vain for proof of this teaching. But the speakers sounded so convincing, and the whole system *kind of* made sense. Besides, it was standard evangelical teaching at the time. Everybody pretty much repeated the same teaching on forgiveness, so I decided it must be true. As I started teaching the Bible, I repeated what I had been taught, all the while suppressing those nagging doubts—and hoping that no one would directly ask me the same kind of challenging questions I felt deep inside. I could only offer them the same lame explanations I had been given.

Not knowing any alternative, I tried "keeping short accounts with God." What were we supposed to do to accomplish this? We were told to spend time in introspection and ask the Holy Spirit to reveal any-thing in our lives that was wrong. Then we were to confess these fail-ings to the Lord and ask his forgiveness. We would then be "cleansed" of our sins, and God would again be willing to hear our prayers. This was crucial because, as we were taught, "If you have any unconfessed sins in your life, God will not hear your prayers." With such a terrible consequence threatened against us, naturally we went about trying to keep those "accounts" of our sins as short as possible!

And all the while, we were also being taught with conviction to believe that "all our sins are forgiven, past, present, and future"!

I don't know whether you have been taught a view of Christian liv-ing like this, but whether you have or haven't, I ask you: Under this kind of teaching, what would you as a believer concentrate on? On Jesus Christ and his wonderful promises, or upon *yourself* and your own performance? Obviously, it would be the second. All you *can* do under teaching like this, if you take it seriously, is to turn inward and concentrate on what *you are doing* rather than on what Christ has done.

Focusing attention on what you are doing and believing God's acceptance is based on your performance is the short road back to legalism, with all its consequences.

Forgiveness—A Means to God's Goal

After discovering that this whole system of "staying in fellowship with God" and "keeping short accounts" with him is not taught in the New Testament, I became open to new insights and to rethinking my whole understanding. One of the passages that helped open my eyes was 2 Corinthians 5:18-19:

> All this is from God, who reconciled us to himself through Christ and gave us the ministry of reconciliation: that God was reconciling the world to himself in Christ, not counting people's sins against them. And he has committed to us the message of reconciliation.

This concept of "reconciliation" jumped out at me like neon. In these verses Paul is describing God's purpose in sending Christ to die for us. It was to *reconcile* us; in fact, to reconcile *the whole world* to himself. How did he accomplish it? By "not counting people's sins against them"—which is simply saying in other words, forgiving them. This observation hit me like a hammer blow. From God's perspective, *forgiveness is not an end in itself; forgiveness is the necessary means to reconciliation*. It was *reconciliation with man* that God desired, and Christ's death to accomplish our forgiveness was the means.

Thinking this through from the standpoint of human relations, it made sense. If two people get into a conflict, when would you say the problem has been truly solved? Let's say the offended party says, "Okay, I forgive him, but I never want to see or talk to him again." Is that a true solution? No, of course not. Apart from a desire for reconciliation, "forgiving him" changes nothing about the situation. Reconciliation may not always be possible in this fallen world, but it is the proper goal of forgiveness.

The same is true between God and mankind. Therefore, God had to accomplish a complete and final forgiveness if his desire was to reconcile us to himself. Praise the Lord, that's exactly what he did through Jesus Christ! Christ's death accomplished total forgiveness for us ("not counting people's sins against them") so that we could be brought back into a free and loving relationship with God (made possible by our reconciliation). With this goal in mind, God could not have offered only a "partial forgiveness." Forgiveness had to be complete and once-and-for-all, or reconciliation would not be possible.

The gospel, therefore, is not a promise of what God *will do* if you put your faith in Christ. It is an announcement of *what God has done* through Christ and an offer for all men, women, boys, and girls to receive this accomplished reconciliation as a free gift through faith alone in Christ:

> We are therefore Christ's ambassadors, as though God were making his appeal through us. We implore you on Christ's behalf: Be reconciled to God. God made him who had no sin to be sin for us, so that in him we might become the righteousness of God (2 Corinthians 5:20-21).

When Paul calls on people to "be reconciled to God," he is essentially saying, "God has built a bridge from the human race back to himself. The bridge is Christ and the complete forgiveness he has accomplished. Believe the good news, and come back to God as your Father through him."

I'm sure you've had the experience of having something called to your attention—a new model of car, for example. Before that time, you were unaware of it. Now, it seems you see that new model every time you're out on the road. Nothing has really changed except your awareness of it. That's the way the concept of reconciliation worked with me.

Paul addressed the concept in another passage where you see the same connection:

> God was pleased to have all his fullness dwell in him, and through him to *reconcile* to himself all things, whether things on earth or things in heaven, *by making peace through his blood, shed on the cross.*
>
> Once you were alienated from God and were enemies in your minds because of your evil behavior. But now he has *reconciled you by Christ's physical body through death* to present you holy in his sight, without blemish and free from accusation (Colossians 1:19-22).

Once again, Christ's death, "making peace through his blood, shed on the cross," is the means to reconciliation.

This is the biblical teaching that first began to unlock my understanding. I wrote a Bible study booklet at the time and changed my approach in teaching seminars to boldly proclaim the centrality of reconciliation, and how it demanded a total forgiveness given to us in Christ. People perked up their ears like I'd never seen before, and many were deeply impacted by it.

This is it, I thought. *I've got it now, I've got the key.* Yes, I had one of the keys, but this was only the first step of my journey to New Covenant conviction. More steps were to follow, and the pace became more rapid.

Contrasting Law and Grace

When you receive life-changing insights, you naturally start to eagerly track down other people who have seen the same. Though these insights were new to me, I found they had been discovered and taught by many wonderful Bible teachers through the centuries. It also seemed that after the passing of those teachers, their insights fell into neglect and were eventually forgotten. Perhaps God has determined that each generation must discover them for themselves.

Following my study of reconciliation and its implications, I began to find references to "law and grace." To remind you of what was said in the previous chapter, to discuss *law* meaningfully, you have to specify which meaning of the word you're using in the context. *The Law* as a *covenant* refers to the Law of Moses, the whole body of commandments taught from Exodus to Deuteronomy; what we call the Old Covenant. However, *law* as a *principle* can be any system of works, God-given or man-made, by which a person attempts to earn or maintain the acceptance of God.

It never occurred to me to try to live by the Mosaic Law. After all, I didn't live in the Old Testament period, and I was not a Jew. It also did not occur to me that I might still be "living by law" in the sense of a principle. I had not heard of that possibility, and looking back, I don't believe I ever heard anyone teach on the subject.

Now, however, in my pursuit of greater understanding of reconciliation and total forgiveness, I began to come across teachers of the past who talked in various ways about "law and grace." I became intrigued and looked for more, and found that this theme kept popping up through the Christian centuries, whenever there was a revival of understanding about the grace of God.

Augustine, who lived 1600 years ago, wrote a work called *Of the Spirit and the Letter* (inspired by Paul's discussion in 2 Corinthians 3), in which he described how these two principles are opposed to each other, and that God wants us to live in the motivation and power of his grace. A thousand years later, Martin Luther made "law and gospel" (his term for what I call "law and grace") the heart of his teaching.

He was so convinced that this distinction is central to Christian understanding that he pronounced it necessary for accurate biblical teaching: "Hence, whoever knows well this art of distinguishing between law and gospel, place him at the head and call him a doctor of Holy Scripture." In the late nineteenth and the twentieth century, teachers like C.I. Scofield and Lewis Sperry Chafer were strong proponents of understanding law and grace.

God's Answer to the Law Problem

The principles of law and grace are in opposition to one another. Remember that as far as their practical results in people's lives, there is no difference between "Law" as a covenant and "law" as a principle. Therefore biblical passages that refer primarily to the Law of Moses can be used to illustrate the principle of law and its effects in application.

The Bible makes clear the role of the Law and how the gospel is the answer:

> All who rely on the works of the law are under a curse, as it is written, "Cursed is everyone who does not continue to do everything written in the Book of the Law." Clearly no one who relies on the law is justified before God, because "the righteous will live by faith." The law is not based on faith; on the contrary, it says, "The person who does these things will live by them" (Galatians 3:10-12).

> The law was our guardian until Christ came that we might be justified by faith. Now that this faith has come, we are no longer under a guardian (Galatians 3:24-25).

Quoting the Old Testament Scriptures, Paul demonstrates that the effect of God's Law on the individual was to place him or her under a "curse." Why? Because to be "justified" before God (have a standing of complete righteousness) would require keeping "*everything* written in the Book of the Law." God doesn't grade on the curve. If he evaluated us according to the principle of law, we would all fail, because the only passing grade is 100 percent perfection.

Why would God give us a standard that we cannot keep and that results in our being cursed? *So we will come to understand our need for a Savior and be prepared to hear the gospel.* Paul says, "Now that this faith has come, we are no longer under a guardian," which was the Law. The work of the Law is to declare God's standard and to convict us of our failure. When we come to this knowledge, the Law has done its job. Then through the gospel of grace we come to faith in Christ. From that point on, God does not intend us to try to live according to law.

To summarize the principles, it helps to see law and grace in contrast. Law is God prohibiting and requiring. Grace is God graciously giving what his own holiness demands. Law is mankind trying to earn and maintain God's acceptance. Grace is God giving that perfect acceptance. Law is what man can do in his own unaided strength. Grace is about God giving us a heart to respond and the power to please and serve him. Law is God commanding us to love him and our neighbor. Grace is God first loving us (1 John 4:19), which causes us to love him. Then he says, "As I have loved you, so you must love one another" (John 13:34).

Behind the whole discussion is the good news that the Son of God has come "to seek and to save the lost" (Luke 19:10). As Scofield said, "Under law, sheep died for their shepherd. Under grace, the Good Shepherd died for his sheep."

Discovering law and grace made so many things clear, and I found the whole Bible coming into greater harmony and focus. As I began to teach these things, again I found people responding with greater joy, freedom, and eagerness to learn more.

This is it, I thought. *I've got it now.* But there were more marvelous things to learn.

Our Identity in Christ

Understanding my total forgiveness and reconciliation through the grace of God was already life-changing to me. I found myself softening in my relationships with my wife and children. I began to gain more compassion for them, especially as I began to realize how hard I had been in my "religiosity." Being a "bold witness for Christ" (I thought), I had not only been hard on my staff, as in the "Dragon" story. I did the same to my family too.

There were occasions when my daughter, Debbie, would come home from school and excitedly tell me about making a new friend. "That's great," I often responded. "Did you witness to her?" The thought of that attitude began to make me cringe in embarrassment and regret. Grace was giving me a clearer view of myself.

I found in continued study that as much as forgiveness and reconciliation were discussed in the New Testament, they were not the only major concepts to be found. The apostles used other words to explain the work of Christ to save us: redemption, justification, and sanctification. At first I just thought that these were alternate (and more difficult) ways of explaining the major truth of forgiveness and reconciliation. But I found that this wasn't true.

Redeemed, Justified, Sanctified

When we speak of salvation, I think we sometimes miss how large this truth is. As wonderful as forgiveness is, for example, salvation is a reality far too big for only that term. The reason God uses these other words is because he is teaching us many different perspectives so we can see how wonderful our salvation is. Each one is a word picture to reveal a facet of what Christ has done.

To be *redeemed* is a picture of Christ purchasing us out of the slave market of sin, and making us his own:

> You know that it was not with perishable things such as silver or gold that you were *redeemed* from the empty way of life handed down to you from your ancestors, but with the precious blood of Christ, a lamb without blemish or defect (1 Peter 1:18-19).

To be "justified" (same Greek root word as "righteousness") is a legal concept. The picture is our appearing as defendants before God as Judge and receiving a verdict of complete innocence. A good working definition of justification is that it is "God's work as Judge where he declares a guilty sinner to be totally righteous in his sight, on the basis of Christ's finished work on the cross and that person's faith in him."

> All have sinned and fall short of the glory of God, and all are *justified* freely by his grace through the redemption that came by Christ Jesus...For we maintain that a person is *justified* by faith apart from the works of the law (Romans 3:23-24,28).

To be "sanctified" (same Greek root word as "holy" or "holiness") means to be *set apart as God's special, beloved possession.* It's often mistakenly understood as referring primarily to behavior, but that is not true. When Paul wrote to the church at Corinth, he began with this greeting:

> To the church of God in Corinth, to those *sanctified* in Christ Jesus and called to be *his holy people* (1 Corinthians 1:2).

The phrase "called to be his holy people" can be translated, "called as saints." The word *saint* or *holy one* does not refer to a certain special category of Christian. Every Christian is a saint in God's eyes. It's not a matter of behavior. It's a matter of identity. By *his work* we have been sanctified in God's sight:

> By that will, we have been *made holy* [or *sanctified*] through the sacrifice of the body of Jesus Christ once for all (Hebrews 10:10).

Now of course, God wants us to grow so that our behavior conforms to who we are, but it's not our behavior that makes us who we are. The Corinthians themselves are the ultimate proof. After calling them "sanctified," Paul goes on to write 16 chapters to correct the wrong behaviors and attitudes they have been exhibiting. They might have been misbehaving saints, but they were saints nonetheless!

"In Christ"

Gaining deeper understanding of these great word pictures from the New Testament made me appreciate more and more how great the grace of God is. But what ties them all together? This is where the significance of a very small biblical phrase took on huge value for me: "in Christ."

The concept of being "in" someone may be new to you, but it's very biblical. According to the Scriptures, there are only two kinds of people in the world: those who are "in Adam" and those who are "in Christ." To be "in" someone means that either Adam or Christ is your family head. He determines your heritage, your identity, your nature, and your destiny:

> As in Adam all die, so in Christ all will be made alive
> (1 Corinthians 15:22).

We are all born into this world "in Adam." We are part of his family. "In Adam" is our identity. We possess his fallen nature and its consequences: sin, death, and alienation from God. And unless something changes, we are headed straight toward a destiny where those facts will become eternal.

But those who hear the gospel and believe are transferred *out of Adam* and placed *into Christ*. Water baptism is an outward picture of this spiritual reality that occurs the moment one trusts in Christ as Savior:

> Don't you know that all of us who were baptized *into Christ Jesus* were baptized into his death? We were therefore buried with him through baptism into death in order that, just as Christ was raised from the dead through the glory of the Father, we too may live a new life (Romans 6:3-4).

It's because we are *in Christ* that we possess all that he is and all that he gives. We don't have to live in anxiety, for example, about whether or not we Christians are redeemed and forgiven. Because we are in Christ, these things are facts:

> *In him we have redemption* through his blood, *the forgiveness*
> *of sins,* in accordance with the riches of God's grace that he
> lavished on us (Ephesians 1:7-8).

I realized that for a long time I had come to the Lord as if he were a vending machine. If I needed some forgiveness, I would go to him and he dispensed it, bit by bit. But now I saw that forgiveness is something that is found in Christ, and since I am in Christ I possess forgiveness continually. It's a continuous, present possession. I live in forgiveness just like I live in and breathe the air. Forgiveness and all those other facets of his accomplishment are found *in him.* That is my true identity.

Christ Living in Me

Once again I responded, "That's it! I've got it!" As I put these truths into my teaching, more and more people were responding to learning about the grace of God that is lavished on us. Learning about their identity in Christ was setting scores of believers free to enjoy their relationship with the Lord. But there was one more major piece of the puzzle he wanted to show me.

Over the years I had heard of Major Ian Thomas, an author and Bible teacher who literally traveled the world spreading his message. Once, earlier in my life, I had heard him speak, but left more puzzled than enlightened. I wasn't ready. But in the early 1980s I heard that he was speaking in the Dallas area, and I went to hear him.

This time the message hit me like a lightning bolt. It made perfect sense when he summarized the gospel this way: "Jesus Christ gave his life for you, so that he could give his life to you, so that he could live his life through you." The Christian faith, he said, was not all about a dead Savior—it was about a *living* Christ. His death for us was necessary to clear the decks for the divine action of raising us from the dead spiritually. Why? Because the problem of humanity apart from God is not just that people are guilty sinners in need for forgiveness, though that's true. Human beings are spiritually dead, devoid of the only thing that can make them able to function as God intended: the indwelling life of God himself.

Major Thomas pointed persistently to a key verse of Scripture:

> I have been crucified with Christ and I no longer live, but *Christ lives in me.* The life I now live in the body, I live by faith in the Son of God, who loved me and gave himself for me (Galatians 2:20).

I had understood and taught about the ministry of the Holy Spirit before, but in my thinking it was really all about "power for service." Certainly, the Holy Spirit provides power for service, but that's not all by any means. Through the Holy Spirit, *Christ himself lives in us.* He supplies us life so that we can enjoy a relationship with him. Then, from that life and relationship should flow our Christ-empowered service.

This was the capstone of the new understanding the Lord brought me to. Not that I now "know it all," of course, because I hope to continue learning and deepening in understanding as long as I live. You never get to the end of the Word of God! But this was the final piece of the puzzle that enabled me to arrive at the answer to those prayers fueled by tears. The Lord did "bring me back" to joy, and much more.

What I had discovered was the New Covenant. For the last 25 years, my passion has been to proclaim this message in every way I can.

4

The Glory and Weakness of the Old Covenant

People—Not God—Were the Problem

In 2011, millions of people gathered around their television sets to watch the wedding of Prince William of England and Kate Middleton. The event was a regal spectacle. Anyone watching would have told you that it was no ordinary wedding at all—except for the words spoken by the minister. They were typical of any wedding ceremony. Yes, they were spoken with more pomp and circumstance, but attend another wedding and you'll hear basically the same vows.

Most of us pay very little attention to the words being said at a wedding. We love to hear the bride and groom say their vows to one another. And we do like the kiss. But I would imagine very few people take notice of what is actually transpiring during that joyful occasion. The millions tuned in that day to watch Prince William and Kate tie the knot witnessed a ritual that is as old as mankind: the making of a covenant.

The Elements of a Covenant

A covenant is *a solemn agreement creating a formal relationship between two parties based on specific promises and responsibilities.*

In older times, a covenant could be made between two kings representing two nations, between a king and a subordinate ruler, between two groups such as families or tribes, or between two individuals. And of course, most important for us, God made a covenant between himself and humanity.

Now, covenants differ based on the following three categories. Covenants can be:

1. *Unilateral* or *bilateral.* Unilateral means "one-sided"— that is, all of the duties and responsibilities rest on a *single party* in the agreement. Bilateral means "two-sided"—this means *both* parties have duties and responsibilities in the fulfillment of the covenant.

2. *Unconditional* or *conditional*—In an unconditional covenant, one or both parties are responsible to fulfill their promises regardless of the other party's actions. In a conditional covenant, there is an "if" attached; that is, the covenant is along the lines of, "If you do this, I will do that. But if you don't, I won't." A conditional covenant depends on the performance of the parties involved, and failure to keep the conditions breaks the covenant relationship.

3. *Temporal* or *perpetual*—All covenants have an official beginning, but not all have an ending. A temporal covenant has an end point, some event or time limitation that causes it to come to an end. A perpetual covenant, in contrast, has no end in view. When God is involved, a covenant can continue forever.

The Covenants Found in the Scriptures

The story of the Bible is built upon covenants that God has made with man. Hold a Bible in your hand. As you leaf through it, the first thing you notice is that it is divided into two parts, the Old Testament and the New Testament. The Old Testament includes numerous covenants. The major ones are the Noahic Covenant, the Abrahamic Covenant, the Mosaic or Old Covenant, and the Davidic Covenant. But the one that is most prominent, the one that governs the greatest part of Israel's history, is the Old Covenant, or Mosaic Covenant.

The New Testament is where we find the New Covenant. It was talked about in the Old Testament, but did not take effect until the death of Jesus Christ, as mentioned in chapter 1. These two covenants, the Old and the New, stand in stark contrast to one another. Through this contrast, we see clearly the glory of the New, that it is better and superior in all ways. As a matter of fact, I don't think we can fully appreciate the New Covenant except as it is contrasted with the Old Covenant.

I imagine, like me, you aren't exactly in the habit of buying diamonds, but perhaps you have shopped in a jewelry store a few times. Have you noticed what the sales representatives in jewelry stores do when they show you a gem? They pull out a small pad of black velvet to place it on and hold it under a very bright light. A diamond under bright light against a background of black velvet shines as brightly as it possibly can. It looks like starlight captured in a small container.

The salespeople show the diamond in the best possible light. And I think that's what the Old Covenant does for the New Covenant. It is the black velvet background that displays the New Covenant in all its glory, a glory we would not fully appreciate without it.

The Making of the Old Covenant

I am not exaggerating when I say that this discussion on the Old Covenant is one of the most important passages in this book. It contains some of the most important facts you need to know in order to read and interpret your Bible accurately. I have found that people have never learned, or constantly forget, the biblical truths we will examine. The failure to grasp the following points results in theological confusion and, ultimately, the failure to understand the wonder and glory of the New Covenant.

An Agreement Between God and Israel

First, what is the Old Covenant, which is also known as the Law of Moses? The Law of Moses, or the Old Covenant, is the covenant *between God and the nation of Israel*. It was instituted by God through Moses at Mount Sinai after the exodus from Egypt.

Please don't miss this point: The Law was a covenant between God and *only* the nation of Israel. ***At no time*** *was it ever imposed on any other nation of the world.* I find I have to repeat this again and again. As soon as you turn around, people who've heard this are again arguing that Christians "need to keep the Law." No, they don't. No one but Israel was ever under the Law of Moses.

This is not just because we live in another age. If you read carefully, you will find that nowhere in the Old Testament are the Gentile nations ever commanded to obey the Law; they are not even criticized for not keeping it. The pagan nations are sometimes condemned by the Lord for their arrogant pride, for their idiotic idolatry, or for actions violating the common moral sense the whole human race innately possesses—for excessive cruelty in warfare, for example. But they are never condemned for failing to keep the Law of Moses. The Old Covenant was for Israel alone.

After 20 centuries of Christian history, we are well-accustomed to holding in our hands a single book we call the Bible. The bound unity of the 66 books, while a wonderful blessing to possess, has deceived us to a great extent. Remember, those 66 books were compiled over at least 15 centuries, being penned by as many as 40 different writers. For centuries those books were inscribed on numerous separate scrolls. Only around the third century AD did Christians begin to bind them in a single book. That physical unity blinds people from seeing many of the distinctions within it.

The Bible gives us the history from God's creation of all things to the gradual unfolding of his plan to redeem all mankind from sin and death through Christ. In that gradual unfolding, there were definite stages and changes of conditions. Therefore, to interpret a passage of Scripture accurately, you need to understand the general shape of that unfolding plan, and know what things are different at which times. Thus, the critical questions to ask about any passage are "Who said it to whom?" and "Under what covenant was it said?"

If you don't ask these vital questions, you will tend to read any portion of the Bible and assume it's talking directly to you. But if you are reading from Deuteronomy, for example, the Lord is not talking directly to you. He is talking to the people of Israel living under the Old Covenant.

I know this may raise some questions. Yes, I believe, along with the apostle Paul that "*all* Scripture is God-breathed and is useful for teaching, rebuking, correcting and training in righteousness, so that the servant of God may be thoroughly equipped for every good work" (2 Timothy 3:16-17). However, this presupposes that you have done the preliminary work of discovering what the passage means *in context*. Only after that is it proper to look for a personal application.

Whenever we read anything—book, Internet article, billboard— we have a sense of who it's speaking to, and we relate it to ourselves based on that understanding. The Bible is no different. It is not a book of magical sayings that we can use any way we see fit. We need to have a grasp of who the text is speaking to before we can make proper use of it. With that understanding, we can see that the Law was a covenant only between God and the nation of Israel.

God and His People Enter into Covenant

God initiated the Mosaic covenant after miraculously freeing the people from Egyptian rule. The place was Mount Sinai, in the wilderness. Here is what God proposed:

> Moses went up to God, and the LORD called to him from the mountain and said, "This is what you are to say to the descendants of Jacob and what you are to tell the people of Israel: 'You yourselves have seen what I did to Egypt, and how I carried you on eagles' wings and brought you to myself. Now *if you obey me fully and keep my covenant, then out of all nations you will be my treasured possession.* Although the whole earth is mine, you will be for me a kingdom of priests and a holy nation.' These are the words you are to speak to the Israelites" (Exodus 19:3-6).

In turn,

> Moses went back and summoned the elders of the people and set before them all the words the LORD had commanded

him to speak. The people all responded together, "We will do everything the LORD has said." So Moses brought their answer back to the LORD (verses 7-8).

Notice what God said through Moses:

> Now *if you obey me fully and keep my covenant,* **then** out of all nations you will be my treasured possession (verse 5).

The "if–then" construction marks this covenant as *bilateral* (two-sided) and *conditional.* Both God and Israel will have responsibilities under it.

After Moses took back the people's answer, God commanded the people to prepare themselves and be ritually clean for the ceremony that was to take place on the third day. On that day, accompanied by awesome sights and sounds, the Lord met with Moses and Aaron while the people waited at the foot of the mountain.

This is where God began to spell out the duties and responsibilities of the Covenant, beginning with the Ten Commandments and continuing with an outline of his requirements on a number of religious, social, and personal subjects (Exodus 20–23). Then it was time to ask the people if they would enter this covenant with God:

> When Moses went and told the people all the LORD's words and laws, they responded with one voice, "Everything the LORD has said we will do" (Exodus 24:3).

Moses ratified this covenant through the offering of sacrifices:

> He got up early the next morning and built an altar at the foot of the mountain and set up twelve stone pillars representing the twelve tribes of Israel. Then he sent young Israelite men, and *they offered burnt offerings and sacrificed young bulls* as fellowship offerings to the LORD...Moses then took the blood, sprinkled it on the people and said, *"This is the blood of the covenant* that the LORD has made with you in accordance with all these words" (Exodus 24:4-5,8).

The Extent and Purpose of God's Covenant with Israel

*If you obey me fully and keep my covenant, **then** out of all
nations you will be my treasured possession* (Exodus 19:5).

There is no doubt when God makes a promise, he will keep his side
of this covenant. Therefore, for all practical purposes, you can say that
the terms of the Old Covenant are a human responsibility. It will all
rest on the people's performance. God's responses are spelled out in
great detail. *The Lord offered Israel **earthly blessings** for obedience, and
earthly curses for disobedience.*

If you'd like to read a comprehensive, detailed list of these, I suggest
Deuteronomy 28. I'll summarize it for you. If Israel is faithful and obe-
dient to the covenant, the Lord promises blessings like these: The sky
will rain, their crops will grow, their livestock will multiply, their children will be healthy, and they will win their battles against their enemies. In fact, Israel will be the head of all the nations on earth!

But...if the nation is unfaithful and disobedient to his commandments, the Lord promises curses like these: The sky will not rain, their
crops will not grow, their livestock will not multiply, their children will
be sickly, and they will lose their battles against their enemies. Finally, if
Israel persists in unfaithfulness, they will be scattered all over the globe
and suffer indignities in every other nation on earth.

At this point I will make another assertion that may shock you:
Nowhere *does the Law of Moses offer **eternal life** for obedience.* It is not
even discussed. Look above at the summary of blessings and curses
again: They are all concerned with this life in this world. There is not a
word about going to heaven when you die. There are no threats of eternal judgment after death.

So what was the Law? Why did God give it?

God never intended the Old Covenant as the be-all and end-all.
Taking a big-picture view, the Law was a temporary disciplinary vehicle for the Lord to guide, teach, and protect his people Israel until the
coming of the Redeemer, Jesus Christ.

This is exactly the question raised and answered by Paul in Galatians 3:19:

> Why, then, was the law given at all? It was added because
> of transgressions until the Seed to whom the promise referred
> had come.

In this verse you see both the *purpose* and the *duration* of the Law. Its main purpose is seen in the phrase "because of transgressions." Fallen human beings are sinful. God, knowing that many centuries would pass before the coming of Christ, needed a way to teach and restrain the sinfulness of his people. The Law was both for their instruction and for their protection. No society can survive without civil laws, else lawlessness will cause it to be destroyed from within. That's why Paul says in another place,

> We know that *the law is good if one uses it properly.* We
> also know that *law is made not for the righteous but for
> lawbreakers and rebels, the ungodly and sinful, the unholy
> and irreligious;* for those who kill their fathers or mothers,
> for murderers, for the sexually immoral, for those practicing
> homosexuality, for slave traders and liars and perjurers—
> and for whatever else is contrary to...sound doctrine
> (1 Timothy 1:8-10).

The key thing, however, I would like you to see in Galatians 3:19 is the duration of the Law. It was never meant to last forever. It was meant only to manage God's chosen people "until the Seed to whom the promise referred had come." The "Seed" is a reference to Jesus Christ.

God's Land and God's Presence

So what did the Law do in its time? In the simplest of terms, the Law of Moses describes the conditions under which 1) Israel would be allowed to live in God's land and 2) would enjoy the presence of the Lord living among them—while they waited for God to send the promised Redeemer.

God is eternal, meaning he lives outside the bounds of time. He knew in advance, of course, that Israel would fail. And yet he offered them the possibility of a marvelous, ideal reality: *They were chosen to be the light of the world*. Many people have the mistaken notion that because the Lord had a "chosen people," he must not have cared about the other nations. The truth is exactly the opposite! God cared so much about all the nations that he designated one nation to be his teachers to the world. It's right there in the Law. Moses exhorted the people,

> See, I have taught you decrees and laws as the LORD my God commanded me, so that you may follow them in the land you are entering to take possession of it. Observe them carefully, *for this will show your wisdom and understanding to the nations, who will hear about all these decrees and say, "Surely this great nation is a wise and understanding people"* (Deuteronomy 4:5-6).

The Promised Land given to Israel by God was not located by accident. Look at a map of the world. You'll see that little nation at the junction of the three great land masses of the Eastern Hemisphere: Africa, Asia, and Europe. Israel was perfectly located to reach the world.

It doesn't take much Old Testament knowledge on your part to be aware that Israel was unable to keep the requirements of the Old Covenant. Just shortly after it was ratified, while Moses was on the mountain with God, the people convinced Aaron to fashion an idol, a golden calf. The people bowed down to it and sacrificed to it and said, "These are your gods, Israel, who brought you up out of Egypt." They failed at commandment number one. From this point forward, even though there were many godly individuals who temporarily lifted the culture around them to greater faithfulness, the Old Testament is a record of decline and failure.

For most of Old Testament history, Israel was smack in the middle of the toughest neighborhood in the ancient world. To the south and west was Egypt. To the north and east was a succession of empires in Mesopotamia: Assyria, Babylon, and Persia. Those two centers engaged in centuries of conflict, fighting over who would be the reigning superpower of the time. And right in the middle, like a walnut in the jaws of a giant vise, was Israel. They had God's promise that if they were faithful to the covenant, they could remain independent and unafraid.

However, if they became unfaithful, the Lord would allow that super-power vise to crush them. Their choices would have dramatic and powerful consequences. It was "Be faithful, or be conquered."

The persevering grace of the Lord can be seen century after century as he calls his people back to him, as he sends prophets to express his heart of love for them, as he rescues them time and time again from bondage of their own making. He compares them to an unfaithful wife, and expresses the emotions of a betrayed husband. Still, God proclaims his love for them and implores them to return to him. In the long run, however, they followed after other gods, practiced the degrading "worship" patterns of the pagans, and despised the basic values of justice, mercy, and faithfulness.

Eventually, the Lord allowed Israel to have the consequences he had outlined in his covenant with them. His presence abandoned the Temple. The Northern Kingdom of Israel was given into the hands of the Assyrians, and the Southern Kingdom of Judah was destroyed by the Babylonians. As he had warned, the Lord evicted them from his land. The small remnant that returned lived under foreign domination for five more centuries (with the exception of the Maccabean period), and was still ruled by pagans when the Messiah was born in Bethlehem.

Israel's Failure Makes Room for Something Better

Israel's inability to keep the Old Covenant, however, is cited as one of the reasons for the New Covenant. The writer of Hebrews stated it this way:

> If there had been nothing wrong with that first covenant, no place would have been sought for another (Hebrews 8:7).

The writer is simply saying that if the Law of Moses had been capable of accomplishing all that God wanted to do for us, there never would have been a "new" covenant. The very fact that the New Covenant was promised and then accomplished by Christ proves that there was something inadequate about the old one. While many Christians of the past and present would shrink from making such a straight-forward comment about the Law, the writer of Hebrews felt no such reluctance:

> The former regulation [the Old Covenant] is set aside *because it was **weak** and **useless*** (for the law made nothing perfect), and *a **better hope** is introduced* [the New Covenant], by which we draw near to God (Hebrews 7:18-19).

Having taught these biblical truths to people for over 25 years, I can tell you that to first-time readers, these passages are often genuinely shocking. Many get openly angry. And yet, all I'm doing is reading Bible verses and pointing out what they say. The inherent religiosity of human nature has real trouble grasping the radical grace and truth found in Jesus Christ and his gospel.

Honoring the Law for What It Was

If you find these verses hard to swallow, let me again point out that I am only directing your attention to what the Bible actually says. And along with that, let me add two more points.

First, when you allow the Bible to be what it really is—"the best commentary on the Bible"—you will find that you are not dishonoring the Law of Moses by discovering these things. You are actually *honoring* God's Law, the Old Covenant, by recognizing its real purpose. For example, the apostle Paul clearly states that "no one will be declared righteous [justified] in God's sight by the works of the law" (Romans 3:20), then asserts, "We maintain that a person is justified by faith apart from the works of the law" (verse 28). In saying this, is Paul insulting God's Law? No, he then says,

> Do we, then, nullify the law by this faith? Not at all! Rather, *we uphold the law* (verse 31).

As we have already seen, the major purpose of the Law was to reveal to us our sin and guilt, thereby convincing us of our need for Christ, a Savior who can do for us what we could never do for ourselves. The Law is like a mirror that shows us we have a dirty face. We are not dishonoring it by saying it could not save us, any more than we are dishonoring the mirror by saying it could not wash our face. It was never intended to do so.

Second, when we say that the Law was done away with and superseded by the New Covenant, we are not denying that it was glorious in its time. After all, Paul says this as well:

> If the ministry that brought death [the Old Covenant], which was engraved in letters on stone, *came with* **glory**, so that the Israelites could not look steadily at the face of Moses *because of its* **glory**, transitory though it was…If the ministry that brought condemnation was **glorious**…And if what was transitory came *with* **glory**…(2 Corinthians 3:7,9,11).

We should never underestimate how wonderful it was to possess the true revelation of God in the Law of Moses. Imagine a world of complete spiritual darkness: paganism, "gods" beyond number, human sacrifice, child sacrifice, religious prostitution, degrading and ridiculous myths describing the behavior of the "divine beings"; ignorance, superstition, cruelty, and foolishness in every land. Then God picks out one nation—one people to whom he will reveal himself, and through whom he will work to provide spiritual light to the world. We will see more of what this means as we proceed. For now, let us recognize how precious was this revelation entrusted to Israel.

A bunch of desert nomads who became tribal farmers (in the eyes of other nations) held in their possession greater wisdom and knowledge of the truth than did the magi of Babylon, the priests of Egypt, and the philosophers of Greece *put together.* Looked at through secular eyes, it is almost impossible to explain by natural means how *these* people came to possess this treasure. The only answer: They were chosen by God.

The Greater Glory of the New

I am not saying the Law did not have glory. On the contrary, I am merely saying along with Paul that the glory of the Old Covenant *is far surpassed by the* **greater** *and* **permanent glory** *of the New Covenant*:

> Will not the ministry of the Spirit [the New Covenant] be
> *even more glorious?*...how much *more glorious* is the
> ministry that brings righteousness! For what was glorious has
> no glory now in comparison with the *surpassing glory...how*
> *much greater is the glory of that which lasts!* (2 Corinthians
> 3:8,9,10,11).

In the middle of a dark night, a full moon can shine gloriously, allowing you to find your way safely without the aid of artificial light and even casting shadows on the ground. But what is the glory of the moon once the sun has risen? The glory of the sun so far surpasses that of the moon that you hardly notice the moon in the sky when it's visible in the daytime.

Look at another contrast between the Old and New Covenants:

> The law was given through Moses; grace and truth came
> through Jesus Christ (John 1:17).

The apostle John is not saying there was no grace or truth in the Old Covenant, just as Paul was not saying there was no glory in it. John is merely saying that, while those qualities of God were visible in the Law, they are only brought to full representation in Jesus Christ. He is grace and truth to the nth degree.

For us to fully appreciate the glory of the New Covenant, it's crucial to understand the glory of the Old. We need to clearly see what the Law was, and what the Law was *not*. The outcome of our investigation will be a better understanding of God's work in history, and a deeper appreciation for the complete salvation that has been accomplished by Jesus Christ.

If you come to the place where you say you are a New Covenant man or woman, like me you will give thanks to God for the revelation of the Old Covenant. But at the same time, you'll never want to go back to it by abandoning the privileges and freedom of the New Covenant. What we now have is so much better!

The End of the Old and the Prophecy of the New

Despite the many predictions of impending judgment in the messages of the prophets, the amazing grace of the Lord is always evident. Even as God declares the breaking of the Old Covenant, he invariably points forward to a future day and the making of a covenant that will never fail. What the people could not do on their own, God will accomplish for them by his own power and love.

The principal passage presenting this promise was given through the prophet Jeremiah:

> "The days are coming," declares the LORD, "when I will make a *new covenant* with the people of Israel and with the people of Judah" (Jeremiah 31:31).

There, in the years just preceding the Babylonian captivity—Israel's punishment for their failure to keep the Old Covenant—the Lord looks beyond it and promises the New Covenant. What we can know from this verse is that the announcement of a "new" covenant implies the ending of the "old" covenant. As the writer of Hebrews comments,

> By calling this covenant "new," *he has made the first* obsolete; and what is obsolete and outdated will soon disappear (Hebrews 8:13).

Then, before announcing what the New Covenant will be, the Lord makes clear what it is *not*, and just why he declares the Old Covenant null and void:

> "It will *not be like* the covenant I made with their ancestors when I took them by the hand to lead them out of Egypt, *because they broke my covenant*, though I was a husband to them," declares the LORD (Jeremiah 31:32).

Different and Better

From this one verse, Jeremiah 31:32, you can make a number of important observations. First, the New Covenant will be *different* from the Old Covenant: "It will *not be like* the covenant" God made after the exodus, which clearly refers to the Law of Moses. But second and most important, God declares that Israel has broken the covenant. Remember, the Old Covenant was a *conditional* covenant. It began with an "if." The persistent and gross idolatry the Israelites practiced throughout these centuries is described as "spiritual adultery" by the prophets. The nation was unable to keep their part of the covenant, and it is therefore declared broken and done away with.

Now the Lord is ready to give the gist of the coming New Covenant:

> "This is the covenant I will make with the people of Israel after that time," declares the LORD. "I will put my law in their minds and write it on their hearts. I will be their God, and they will be my people. No longer will they teach their neighbor, or say to one another, 'Know the LORD,' because they will all know me, from the least of them to the greatest," declares the LORD. "For I will forgive their wickedness and will remember their sins no more" (Jeremiah 31:33-34).

You could say that these verses are the entire New Testament in a nutshell. Or, that the New Testament is a comprehensive commentary on the truths contained in these verses. Just like a small acorn contains the complete DNA of the mighty oak that will grow from it, the fully explained New Covenant will grow and expand from this promise.

According to the writer of Hebrews,

> The former regulation [the Old Covenant] is set aside because it was *weak* and *useless* (for the law made nothing perfect), and a *better hope* [the New Covenant] is introduced, by which we draw near to God...Because of [God's] oath, *Jesus has become the guarantor of a **better covenant*** (Hebrews 7:18-19,22).

The Old Covenant has been declared weak, useless, and obsolete. And we have seen that the New Covenant is both *different* and *better* than the Old Covenant.

God Himself Comes to Help

It's time to raise some questions: *Why* was the Old Covenant "weak" and "useless"? We have looked at it from the big picture, historical perspective. What were its purpose and effects on individuals, then and now?

Most important for us who live in this age, in what way is the New Covenant different and better than the Old? What promises are contained in it, and how can we be sure they will come true?

The essence of religion can be described as "man's efforts to reach up to God," but these will always be totally inadequate. The New Covenant of Jesus Christ, however, is about *God's work to reach down to man.* In Isaiah, just after God observed the wretched state of his people and "was appalled that there was no one to intervene," we have this wonderful announcement:

> So **his own arm** worked salvation for him, and **his own righteousness** sustained him. He put on righteousness as his breastplate, and the helmet of salvation on his head; *he put on* the garments of vengeance and wrapped himself in zeal as a cloak (Isaiah 59:16-17).

The Lord himself promises to take action, and this forms one of the earliest New Covenant prophecies:

> "*The Redeemer will come to Zion*, to those in Jacob who repent of their sins," declares the LORD. "As for me, *this is my covenant with them*," says the LORD. "My Spirit, who is on you, will not depart from you, and my words that I have put in your mouth will always be on your lips, on the lips of your children and on the lips of their descendants—from this time on and forever," says the LORD (Isaiah 59:20-21).

The apostle Paul saw these verses as fulfilled in Christ, and quotes them in Romans 11:26-27. These promises exemplify the New Covenant difference. Under the Law of Moses, human beings were held responsible to be faithful for the covenant to be fulfilled. But in the

New Covenant, God himself takes the responsibility to solve the problem. He is the one who will fulfill it.

This is why the New Covenant is superior in every way.

Do you find this as exciting and liberating as I do? I urge you to keep reading. There are more great things to come.

5

The New and Better Covenant
There's No More "If"

One day not long before the writing of this book, I enjoyed a lunch meeting with the People to People staff. As we did often, we got into a discussion of the New Covenant and the difficulty many people have in understanding it.

My wife, Amy, was present, and she commented, "You know what it's like? Many people's understanding is like a big stew pot. Preachers and Bible teachers and other Christians pick out verses from all over the Bible and just toss them into the pot. There's no distinction between the Old Covenant and the New. People end up with a goulash of understanding where it's all blended together and nothing makes sense."

Amy hit the nail right on the head. She's always had a talent for coming up with new and striking illustrations.

Her comments reminded me that Jesus had used two different metaphors to explain the same problem. On one particular occasion some disciples of John the Baptist came and asked the Lord why his disciples did not follow some of the traditional religious practices of the Pharisees and others:

71

Jesus answered…"No one sews a patch of unshrunk cloth
on an old garment, for the patch will pull away from the
garment, making the tear worse" (Matthew 9:15-16).

An old garment has already shrunk through washing and use. If
you patch a hole with a piece of new, unshrunk cloth, it will shrink and
tear away. The garment will be in worse shape than before you "fixed"
it. Jesus continued,

"Neither do people pour new wine into old wineskins. If
they do, the skins will burst; the wine will run out and the
wineskins will be ruined. No, they pour new wine into new
wineskins, and both are preserved" (verse 17).

The first illustration about the cloth is probably clear to you, since
it's the same today, at least with natural fabrics. The one about the
wineskins may need a little explanation. Back then, wine for everyday
use was contained in animal skins. When the wine was fresh and new,
it was always placed in a new wineskin. The reason for this is that the
fermentation process was still continuing, creating gases that caused
expansion. A new wineskin was still elastic enough to stretch along
with that process. However, you would never put new wine into an
old, previously used wineskin. Why? Because it had already stretched
as far as it could and had become dry and brittle. It had no more elastic-
ity. Once the new wine began producing gases causing expansion, the
wineskin would burst. It would be ruined, and the wine would be lost.

Both of these illustrations are making the same point: The New
Covenant cannot be contained within the forms and limits of the Old
Covenant. The Old is represented by the old garment and the old
wineskin. They have already stretched to the limit and have no more
capacity for expansion. However, the New Covenant, represented by
the new patch of cloth and the new wineskin, is alive and expanding
indefinitely.

The Old Covenant and the New Covenant are incompatible. The
effort to mix the two results in the loss of the power of both. The
attempt to blend the two results in an incoherent understanding of the
Bible, as in Amy's illustration of a theological goulash. Understanding

both covenants and keeping them distinct is absolutely necessary to live in the power of what Christ has done for us.

The New Covenant: Different and Better

As we take a closer look at God's promise of the New Covenant, you will see clearly why it and the Old Covenant are incompatible. You will also understand why the New Covenant is described as both *different* and *better* than the Old. I hope as well that this study will enable you to completely entrust yourself to living in the life and power that comes to us through this New Covenant.

Let's look again carefully at what the Lord promised through Jeremiah around 600 years before Christ. This time I will emphasize certain words:

> "This is the covenant *I will* make with the people of Israel after that time," declares the LORD. "*I will* put my law in their minds and write it on their hearts. *I will* be their God, and they will be my people. No longer will they teach their neighbor, or say to one another, 'Know the LORD,' because they will all know me, from the least to the greatest," declares the LORD. "For *I will* forgive their wickedness and will remember their sins no more" (Jeremiah 31:33-34).

*The first important thing to observe about the New Covenant is what it does **not** say.* What is missing? Just one little two-letter word, one word that makes all the difference in the world: *There is no "if."* As I often say, we're not in the equation here!

Concerning the promises and provisions of this New Covenant, God says, "I will…I will…I will…I will." The responsibility rests completely on his shoulders. There is not a single responsibility placed on man. Nowhere! Before we read any further, we can already identify the New Covenant as *unconditional*, because of the lack of an "if," and *unilateral*, because all the responsibility is assumed by God. We're not in the equation. And if these things are true, we can anticipate that this New Covenant will also be *perpetual*—eternal and unending—because without the possibility of human failure ending it, we can be confident the Lord's promises will never fail because he is eternal and unending.

So even before we examine the individual clauses in this promise, the big picture already tells us how the New Covenant is both different and better than the Old.

The Old Covenant was *conditional, bilateral,* and *temporal.* It was based on the performance of Israel, beginning with "*If* you obey me fully and keep my covenant," making it conditional. It contained duties and responsibilities on the part of both God and man, making it bilateral—two-sided. And because it depended on the performance of human beings, it certainly had the possibility of failure, making it temporal. We know now in hindsight, of course, that the Lord never intended it to last forever—only until the coming of Christ. We'll come back later and look at the New Testament passages that teach this.

The New Covenant, on the other hand, is *unconditional, unilateral,* and *eternal.* God says "I will" in regard to all its clauses, making it unconditional. All the duties and responsibilities are assumed by the Lord, making it unilateral—one-sided. And since God's promises never fail, these promises are eternal.

Once more, let me point out this striking contrast: How could a *conditional, bilateral,* and *temporal* covenant ever be mixed and blended with a covenant that is *unconditional, unilateral,* and *eternal*? That's why teachers and students who select verses from all over the Bible without taking into account the different covenants end up creating an indigestible theological goulash. That's why people continue to believe that the Bible contradicts itself. And that's why so many believers are living in confusion instead of in the joy, confidence, and power of New Covenant truth.

Never in history have these two covenants been in force at the same time. And they never will be.

Breaking Down the Promises of the New Covenant

I suggested in the last chapter that Jeremiah's promise of the New Covenant can be described as the whole New Testament in a nutshell—that it contains in seed form everything that the apostles and prophets of the New Testament will reveal, expound, and take to its logical conclusion. Let's look at this prophecy and break it down, with particular attention to drawing out how this New Covenant is both different and better than the Old.

The Issue of Motivation and Power

> I will put my law in their minds and write it on their hearts (Jeremiah 31:33).

To discover how this promise is different and better than the Old, we must first know where and how the Old Covenant was written. Notice first the word *law*—not *laws*, like the Ten Commandments. Keep in mind that this new law is the law of love. In regard to the laws given through Moses, Paul tells us:

> If the ministry *that brought death, which was engraved in letters on stone,* came with glory... (2 Corinthians 3:7).

The apostle is referring to this event:

> When the LORD finished speaking to Moses on Mount Sinai, he gave him the two tablets of the covenant law, the tablets of stone inscribed by the finger of God (Exodus 31:18).

On those stone tablets were written the Ten Commandments, the foundation of the Law of Moses. If you keep reading in Exodus from this point, you'll find that the people of Israel violated their covenant with God even before Moses came down the mountain with the tablets! Moses was so incensed at finding them dancing around the golden calves they had ordered Aaron to make that he smashed the tablets to pieces. The Lord later engraved a second set, which was placed inside the Ark of the Covenant.

The Law was without question the Word of God, being inscribed by his very finger on the stones. It expressed his will for the people of Israel clearly, and demanded their obedience.

More than outward obedience

Beyond what is said above, the Lord makes clear throughout the Old Testament that he wanted much more than mere outward obedience to the letter of the Law. The heart of the Law was expressed in a passage also quoted by Jesus Christ:

> Hear, O Israel: The LORD our God, the LORD is one. Love the LORD your God with all your heart and with all your soul and with all your strength (Deuteronomy 6:4-5).

This passage is known as the *Shema*, Hebrew for "hear," and has been the basic statement of faith of Judaism down to this very day. The Lord Jesus declared that this command, along with the command to "love your neighbor as yourself," were the greatest commandments in the Law. "There is no commandment greater than these," he said (Mark 12:29-31).

However, love is a matter not just of outward actions, but of the heart. That's why, immediately after the *Shema*, the Lord added,

> These commandments that I give you today are to be *on your hearts* (Deuteronomy 6:6).

God looks on the heart

Throughout the Old Testament, in the Law and in the writings of the prophets, we find this emphasis on the heart. When the Lord sent the prophet Samuel to find the new king chosen by God to replace the failed King Saul, he warned him against focusing on men's exterior appearance. At first Samuel was impressed by Eliab, the eldest son of Jesse, but the Lord spoke to him:

> Do not consider his appearance or his height, for I have rejected him. The LORD does not look at the things people look at. People look at the outward appearance, *but the LORD looks at the heart* (1 Samuel 16:7).

When the Lord selected David, it was not because of his intelligence, strength, or appearance—all the things we tend to measure and value. He chose David because of his faith and love for him from the heart.

This emphasis was there in the Law from the beginning, when the Lord included this command:

> Circumcise your **hearts**, therefore, and do not be stiff-necked any longer (Deuteronomy 10:16).

As with baptism in our time, the physical rite of circumcision was not the most important thing. It was meant to be an outward sign of an inward reality. This phrase "circumcise your hearts" can be understood by looking at its opposite, which the Lord specified—he said, "Do not be stiff-necked." To be stiff-necked means to be stubbornly rebellious and hard-hearted toward God. Therefore, to have a circumcised heart would mean to trust in the Lord and obey him from a heart that loves him.

David knew this. This is why he was one of the most remarkable believing persons in the Old Testament. We have a glimpse of his insight in this psalm:

> Sacrifice and offering you did not desire—but my ears you have opened—burnt offerings and sin offerings you did not require. Then I said, "Here I am, I have come—it is written about me in the scroll. *I desire to do your will, my God; your law is within my heart*" (Psalm 40:6-8).

If you take these words literally, David was incorrect. God *did* require sacrifices and offerings. The Law commanded them, and they were in no way optional. But David was able to look through those things and see what God *really* wanted. God wanted the love and faith of people, not the mere outward forms of worship. Only when people approached him with genuine hearts did the Lord find those sacrifices acceptable.

The Law gives commands, but no power

Unfortunately, the history of both the Old and New Testament periods provides abundant proof that human beings can fulfill all the outward signs and procedures demanded by religion without any internal reality at all. *Hypocrisy* comes from the ancient Greek word for an actor, someone who wears a mask on the outside without sincere reality on the inside. This is what the apostle Paul was attacking when he wrote,

> A person is not a Jew who is one only outwardly, nor is circumcision merely outward and physical. No, a person is a Jew who is one *inwardly*; and circumcision is *circumcision of the **heart**,* by the Spirit, not by the written code. Such a person's praise is not from other people, but from God (Romans 2:28-29).

Here Paul is hinting at both the problem of the Old Covenant and the solution brought by the New Covenant. In the Law, God *commanded* the Israelites to circumcise their hearts. He *commanded* them to love him. What was the problem? While the Law could accurately express the will of God and command obedience to it, the Law gave no one the *power* to keep it.

That's why the Old Testament is record upon record of human failure. Even David, who knew these things, was unable to live up to the Law, as the biblical record shows. His notorious sins of adultery and conspiracy to commit murder are recounted in sad detail. It makes you pause: If even the one described as "a man after God's own heart" failed, how could you or I hope to do better?

We need God to do for us what we are incapable of doing for ourselves. This he promises to do in the New Covenant: "I will put my law in their minds and write it on their hearts." (Again, notice the singular "law" referring to the law of love.) As Paul says above, what we need is a "circumcision of the heart, *by the Spirit*, not by the written code." The "written code" (or, the "letter of the Law") could order us to obey God's commands, but that is not enough. *We need the life and power of God himself, "the Spirit,"* to be the people he wants us to be.

In short, *we need a new heart.* We need new motivation from within. We must be changed inwardly by God before we will "delight to do his will," as David wrote.

Under the Old Covenant, humanity's nature and heart remained unchanged. Therefore, the people of Israel were chiefly motivated *extrinsically*, from the outside—that is, through rewards and punishments.

That's why the Law speaks so much about offering earthly blessings for obedience and earthly curses for disobedience. It's the standard way of appealing to people who have only fallen natures, minds, and hearts.

Under the New Covenant, God says his people will be motivated *intrinsically*, from the inside—that is, they will love and serve God *because they want to*. Under the New Covenant, God unilaterally, unconditionally declares that he will give us *new hearts*. He gives us new life. Our natures, minds, and hearts will be transformed. We will be motivated and empowered from within by his Holy Spirit.

The Issue of Relationship

> I will be their God, and they will be my people (Jeremiah 31:33).

This second clause in the announcement of the coming New Covenant sounds almost exactly like what the Old Covenant said. *Almost exactly*. By this time, I'll bet you know what little two-letter word makes the difference. In proposing the Law, the Lord had said,

> *If* you obey me fully and keep my covenant, then out of all the nations you will be my treasured possession. Although the whole earth is mine, you will be for me a kingdom of priests and a holy nation (Exodus 19:5-6).

Israel's status as the chosen people of God was dependent upon their faithfulness to the covenant, as I've pointed out before. And Israel was not faithful. Though the Lord threatened them with the punishments outlined in the Law through dozens of prophets over hundreds of years, they never completely put away their idols, nor did they practice the social justice the Law demanded. God's judgment finally fell on them.

God's consistent desire

Because of the thundering of the prophets and the fearsomeness of those judgments, many people have gotten a wrong idea about the Bible. You'll read this in national news magazines, see it in Internet forums, and hear it repeated on television programs, sometimes by those labeled as "scholars." They say, "There are actually two Gods presented in the Bible: A primitive Old Testament God of wrath and judgment, and an advanced God of love and grace in the New Testament, the Father of Jesus Christ."

Nothing could be further from the truth! There is only one God, and his character is exactly the same from Genesis to Revelation. People who derive that erroneous conclusion from their Bibles are either reading selectively, or they are failing to understand what they are reading. The God you see revealed and dealing with man in the Old Testament is a God full of grace, compassion, forgiveness, and patience. He bore with Israel's persistent sins and unfaithfulness for many generations. He announced his grief over their cold hearts and grossly evil behavior. He pled with them through the prophets. He warned them of the judgment that must come because the covenant demanded it. He restrained his judgment time after time, but ultimately he had to deal with his people in truth and justice. The judgment had to fall.

The God of the Old Testament is no different from the God of the New Testament. No, the thing that makes the Old Testament look so strikingly different from the New Testament is the difference in covenant. While God has not changed—his nature and character being eternal and unchangeable—*his methods of dealing with mankind have clearly changed.* Previously, Israel was under Law, and the Gentiles were left to their own devices. Of all the changes, none is more striking than the shift between the Old and New Covenants.

Remember, the Old Covenant between God and Israel was *conditional* and *bilateral.* It was dependent upon the people's faithfulness and obedience, as Jeremiah reminded them:

> This is the word that came to Jeremiah from the LORD: "Listen to the terms of this covenant and tell them to the people of Judah and to those who live in Jerusalem. Tell them that this is what the LORD, the God of Israel, says: *'Cursed is the man who does not obey the terms of this covenant*—the terms I commanded your ancestors when I brought them out of Egypt, out of the iron-smelting furnace.' I said, *'Obey me*

*and do everything I command you, and you will be my
people, and I will be your God'"* (Jeremiah 11:1-4).

Israel was unable to keep their side of the bargain, so the prophet
announced the covenant's end:

"From the time I brought your ancestors up from Egypt until
today, I warned them again and again, saying, 'Obey me.'
But they did not listen or pay attention; instead, they followed
the stubbornness of their evil hearts. *So I brought on them all
the curses of the covenant* I had commanded them to follow
but that they did not keep" (verses 7-8).

Israel failed. The covenant was broken. The relationship was broken.

Now comes the good news: The Lord promises the coming of a
New Covenant in which he declares, "I will be their God, and they will
be my people." What is most wonderful about this promise, again, is
what *isn't* there: *There is no "if"!*

If our relationship with God depended upon *us*, we would have no
more hope of maintaining it than Israel did. That is, there would be no
hope. None of us is good enough, faithful enough, or pure enough to
merit a relationship with the Lord. We wouldn't be good enough even
if it depended on only the single best day of our lives.

But here God says *he* will do what we could never attain on our own.
It is *not* "*if* we obey him fully and keep his covenant, *then* he will be our
God and we will be his people." *He takes upon himself the responsibility
for our relationship.* He will create and maintain our relationship with
him, based on his own faithfulness to his promise.

There you see the foundation of any sense of real security we can
have. Our relationship does not depend on our faithfulness to him, but
on his faithfulness to us!

The Issue of Access to God

No longer will they teach their neighbor, or say to one
another, "Know the LORD," because they will all know me,
from the least of them to the greatest (Jeremiah 31:34).

This promise of the New Covenant is truly in seed form, and it will later be developed in many remarkable ways in the New Testament. From this early standpoint, we could already guess some of its implications. It seems to be saying, first, that a personal knowledge of the Lord will be granted to everyone. And second, that this knowledge will not be graded according to "status." It will be granted equally to all.

Once again, the difference from the Old Covenant is striking. Even though Israel was God's chosen people, the privileges of service and access into his presence were not given equally by any means.

How different is this New Covenant, in which God says, "*They will all know me, from the least of them to the greatest*"! How much better it is to live under it, through which we all have equal access into the presence of God. As the writer of Hebrews says,

> Let us then approach God's throne of grace with confidence, so that we may receive mercy and find grace to help us in our time of need (Hebrews 4:16).

This great privilege belongs to everyone who is a child of God through faith in Jesus Christ!

The Issue of Forgiveness and Acceptance

> I will forgive their wickedness and will remember their sins no more (Jeremiah 31:34).

I have already emphasized that the God you find in the Old Testament is exactly the same as the God you find in the person of Jesus Christ. His nature and character have not changed. There are many Old Testament passages that celebrate the grace, faithful love, compassion, and forgiveness of the Lord. For example:

> The LORD is compassionate and gracious, slow to anger, abounding in love. He will not always accuse, nor will he harbor his anger forever; he does not treat us as our sins deserve or repay us according to our iniquities. For as high as the heavens are above the earth, so great is his love for

those who fear him; as far as the east is from the west, so far
has he removed our transgressions from us (Psalm 103:8-12).

That is as good and clear an expression of God's love and grace as you can find anywhere in the Bible. To the one who "fears" him—that is, a person of faith—the Lord has always shown his amazing grace and forgiveness. No, the Lord has not changed, but his methods of dealing with mankind have definitely changed. The issue of forgiveness is one clear example. There was forgiveness in the Old Testament, but it is dispensed differently in the New Covenant age.

Elementary instruction

When the Lord was dealing with Israel, he was putting his people through "elementary school." Remember what the world was like before the calling of Israel: dark, ignorant, vile, and often violent paganism everywhere. By choosing this one nation, God was in effect starting from scratch in teaching the world about himself.

Through the Old Covenant, Israel was made aware of God's unapproachable holiness, which was reinforced by the whole system of priesthood and sacrifices, and all this was a continual reminder that there was an unbridgeable gap between God and man.

The system of sacrifices taught several lessons:

- For people to approach a holy God involved specific, extremely exacting procedures, and was not to be attempted lightly.
- God was loving and gracious enough to want a relationship with man, but forgiveness came at a price: "Without the shedding of blood there is no forgiveness" (Hebrews 9:22).
- The price of forgiveness is the death of a sinless substitute.
- Because those sacrifices were made day after day, year after year, a totally adequate sacrifice had not yet appeared. The gap remained and the need continued because "it is impossible for the blood of bulls and goats to take away sins" (Hebrews 10:4).

- The continual need for more sacrifices emphasized that, at
  best, those offerings could cover only *past* sins. *There is no
  sacrifice anywhere in the Law that covers future sins.* Therefore, there could never be once-and-for-all forgiveness
  under the Old Covenant. At best you might be forgiven
  "up to date," but not beyond.

As we have seen, this system ultimately failed. It was never intended
to provide a final solution to the problem of man's sins. The covenant
was broken.

But now, in the promise of the New Covenant, God says, "I will
forgive their wickedness and will remember their sins no more." There
is no "if"; there are no conditions. Just "I will." Forgiveness under this
New Covenant is a given, based on the character of God himself. He
will keep his promise regardless of anything else.

How and when he will institute this New Covenant, it doesn't say.
Israel would have to wait six more centuries, until the coming of Christ,
for the answers to be revealed.

We have taken a bird's-eye view of the promise of the New Covenant. In the chapters ahead we will come down to earth and discover
how the apostles and prophets of the New Testament expound on these
truths, and we'll observe how our riches in Christ grow and develop
from these seeds.

There are many natural questions I have saved until this point in
the book:

- The promises were announced for "the people of Israel and
  with the people of Judah" (Jeremiah 31:31). What about
  the rest of the world?

- The covenant is based in every case on God saying, "I
  will." There are no conditions or duties required of human
  beings. Who does the Covenant apply to? How does one
  get in on it?

- We have seen that the making of a covenant requires an
  official enactment, some action that makes it "legal." What
  will put this covenant into effect?

- We are left with a *curse* placed on Israel because they broke the Old Covenant. What will happen to that curse? How can it be done away with so they can be free to enter into the New Covenant?

We'll begin working through these questions and more in the next chapter.

6

"God's Dividing Line of History"
Jesus Changes Everything

It must have been incredibly exciting, thoroughly confusing, and strangely frightening to be one of Jesus' disciples on the night before his death. On the exciting side, Jesus spoke of the coming of God's kingdom, the great hope of Israel for centuries:

> He said to them, "I have eagerly desired to eat this Passover with you before I suffer. For I tell you, I will not eat it again until it finds fulfillment in the kingdom of God."
>
> After taking the cup, he gave thanks and said, "Take this and divide it among you. For I tell you I will not drink again from the fruit of the vine until the kingdom of God comes" (Luke 22:15-18).

The prophets had written extensively about this future kingdom, not only for Israel, but for the whole earth. Israel would be freed from foreign domination, yes, but much more than that. Universal peace would be established, and all peoples of the world would acknowledge the Lord as God. The lion would lie down with the lamb. Nations would destroy their weapons of war and turn their energies to farming and peaceful pursuits. Even Israel's ancient enemies, Assyria and Egypt, would join her in worshipping the Lord side by side. The curse placed on the earth would be reversed, and God would reign in the person of his King, the Messiah. And all these promises were linked with God's promises to make a New Covenant!

Four centuries of prophetic silence had come to an end with the cry of John the Baptist: "Repent, for the kingdom of heaven has come near" (Matthew 3:2). After being baptized by John, Jesus took up the same proclamation: "Repent, for the kingdom of heaven has come near" (Matthew 4:17). When Jesus later sent his disciples out on a mission, he gave them the same message to announce (Matthew 10:7).

Now, Jesus was saying he would not eat or drink again before the kingdom had come. What did that mean? Perhaps the kingdom was no more than a few days away, the disciples must have thought.

We read these accounts today with full understanding and 2000 years of hindsight to work with. If you think I'm exaggerating the disciples' confusion at this point, notice that even after Jesus' death and resurrection, they asked him right before he ascended into heaven, "Lord, are you *at this time* going to restore the kingdom to Israel?" (Acts 1:6). The kingdom is what they expected, and Jesus' story was not unfolding as they anticipated. On this night it sounded like the kingdom was right around the corner.

Announcement of the New Covenant

On the frightening side, however, were Jesus' ominous words "before I suffer." Certainly, his tone was sober and serious. Whatever he meant, it didn't sound good. He had told them repeatedly on the way to Jerusalem that he would be crucified and rise again the third day, but they did not comprehend him. Today, of course, we know that Jesus' death and resurrection are the very center and foundation of our faith; but again, that's with the benefit of full understanding and hindsight.

The disciples' sense of foreboding could only have deepened when Jesus took common elements of the Passover meal and invested them with new meaning:

> He took bread, gave thanks and broke it, and gave it to them, saying, "This is my body given for you; do this in remembrance of me" (Luke 22:19).

Despite the many question marks in their minds, the disciples could not have missed the significance of the Lord's next words:

> In the same way, after the supper he took the cup, saying, "This cup is the *new covenant* in my blood, which is poured out for you" (Luke 22:20).

They must have felt a thrill of excitement mixed with their confused fear at his reference to "the new covenant." What God had promised through the prophets was here.

The Event That Put the New Covenant into Effect

Just from the words of Luke 22:20 it is possible to identify what event will inaugurate the New Covenant. The reference to Jesus' blood that would be "poured out" can only be a reference to his death. Let me remind you of the principle that applies to a last will and testament:

> In the case of a will, it is necessary to prove the death of the one who made it, because a will is in force only when somebody has died; it never takes effect while the one who made it is living (Hebrews 9:16-17).

When God promised the New Covenant, he performed some of the standard steps of making a covenant. We see first in Jeremiah's prophecy a *statement of purpose*: God announces that he will make a New Covenant because the people could not meet the demands of the Old Covenant. Second, we see in outline form a description of the *duties and responsibilities* of the covenant. In the previous chapter we examined those duties and responsibilities and found that they are all on God's side. They are unilateral, unconditional promises. Israel was unfaithful and broke the Old Covenant, so God would initiate a new one and guarantee its success. However, the Lord did not announce through Jeremiah what would be the *official enactment* of the covenant—that is, what event would make it "legal."

At this final meal with his disciples, Jesus has revealed the answer. His death on the cross will inaugurate the New Covenant. As with a last will and testament, his death will put this covenant into effect.

Remember, in the ancient world it was customary when making covenants to inaugurate them through blood sacrifice. Commenting on this, the writer of Hebrews says,

> This is why even the first covenant was not put into effect without blood. When Moses had proclaimed every commandment of the law to all the people, he took the blood of calves...He said, "This is the blood of the covenant, which God has commanded you to keep" (Hebrews 9:18-20).

If it was necessary from God's point of view to go through this rigorous procedure to create an earthly covenant that was always meant to be temporary, how much more would his *eternal, unconditional, unilateral* covenant require an adequate sacrifice! As Hebrews continues:

> It was necessary, then, for the copies of the heavenly things to be purified with these sacrifices, but the heavenly things themselves with *better sacrifices* than these. For Christ did not enter a sanctuary made with human hands that was only a copy of the true one; he entered heaven itself, now to appear for us in God's presence (Hebrews 9:23-24).

It is impossible to compare the infinite value of the blood of the Son of God with anything on this earth. Because of that infinite value, what he accomplished by his death is also immeasurable:

> He did not enter by means of the blood of goats and calves; but he entered the Most Holy Place once for all *by his own blood*, thus obtaining *eternal redemption* (Hebrews 9:12).

These truths and the ramifications that follow from them are all anticipated in Jesus' brief words, "This cup is the new covenant in my blood, which is poured out for you."

Before we begin our journey to explore the immense ramifications of Jesus' death and the New Covenant, we have some important loose ends to tie up. First of all, we are left with a curse placed on Israel because they broke the Old Covenant. What will happen to that curse? How can it be done away with so Israel can be free to enter into the New Covenant?

This is not only a loose end for us. This was a major bit of unfinished business for God.

Removing the Curse of the Law

The apostle Paul traveled through what is today the central part of the nation of Turkey preaching the gospel. Thousands believed the good news and were converted to Christ. Later, as happened so often, teachers who opposed Paul's gospel followed him through the area, telling those believers that faith in Christ was not enough—they needed to be circumcised and take on the entire way of life commanded under the Law. In short, these teachers were saying that Gentile believers needed to come under the Old Covenant in order to get in on the new one.

Paul vigorously opposed this error, and he wrote his letter to the Galatians to refute it. Part of his strategy to lay out the truth for them was to clarify what the Law of Moses was all about. For Paul, any Christian who would dream of going back to the Old Covenant obviously doesn't understand it. He challenged them, "Tell me, you who want to be under the law, are you not aware of what the law says?" (Galatians 4:21).

What is he referring to? Earlier in the letter he wrote,

> All who rely on the works of the law are under a *curse*, as it is written: "*Cursed* is everyone who does not continue *to do everything* written in the Book of the Law" (Galatians 3:10).

The end result of the Old Covenant for the people of Israel was a national curse. Here Paul points out that the end result for any individual under the Law is the same. Why? Because there is only one "passing grade" under law, and that is absolute perfect obedience: "to do *everything* written in the Book of the Law." James writes the same thing in his letter:

> Whoever keeps the whole law and yet stumbles *at just one point is guilty of breaking all of it* (James 2:10).

But when you are talking about earning acceptance from a holy God, there is no grading on the curve. God demands nothing less than absolute perfection. Therefore, any individual Israelite who attempted to keep the Law well enough to earn God's acceptance and eternal life didn't have a chance. He would fail and receive the Law's curse.

Salvation by Law?

There is a common misconception about this, even among those who understand the gospel of salvation through faith in Christ alone. Many would say, "Yes, we in the New Testament age are saved by faith in Christ, but in the Old Testament people were saved by keeping the Law." This is as wrong as wrong can be.

First, in chapter 4 we saw that the Law does not offer eternal life for obedience. The issue isn't even mentioned, because all of the Law's blessings and curses are concerned with this life in this world. Second, we've already learned that the Law demands perfect obedience in order to avoid its curse, and no one has ever done this apart from Christ. Third, the Old Testament itself says in straightforward language that no human being was righteous on his or her own. This is the point Paul is trying to make for the Galatians. He then builds on this fact:

> Clearly **no one** who relies on the law is justified before God, because "the righteous will live by faith." The law is not based on faith; on the contrary, it says, "The person who *does* these things will live by them" (Galatians 3:11-12).

By Faith Only

As Paul asserts above, "The law is not based on faith." It's a true either/or. Salvation is *either* through one's works according to law (though we've seen that this cannot be), *or* it is a free gift received through faith. But it cannot be both. You can't "merit grace." Neither can you "earn a free gift." For the Galatians to think they could add works of the Law to the salvation they had already freely received by believing the good news is the ultimate in confusion. But this is what we will always do if we don't come to some convictions regarding the New Covenant.

Just as is the case with legalists throughout Christian history, there were always many Israelites who misunderstood and misused the Law to try to be "good enough" to gain God's acceptance. The Pharisees of Jesus' time are a prime example. However, it was *always* improper to try to use the Law as a "ladder" to climb up to earn the acceptance of God. God never intended the Law to be used that way.

On the other hand, the Law was used properly in two ways: 1) when it was used as a "lens" through which to see God and learn about his character, and 2) when it was used as a "mirror" in which people could view themselves in comparison to the character of God because he looks upon the heart. Used in these legitimate ways, the Law worked to lead people to faith in the God of Israel by convicting them of their sins and convincing them of their need for grace. Those who saw this truth and threw themselves on the Lord's mercy and forgiveness through Jesus Christ by faith were justified and accepted by God.

God Does Away with the Curse

Looking at the matter historically, however, we are left with the question of the *national curse* that remained on Israel because of their unfaithfulness to the Old Covenant. Paul seems to have the attitude, "You Gentiles don't know how fortunate you are *not* to be under the Old Covenant!" Now he is ready to explain God's answer to the Law's curse:

> Christ redeemed us from the curse of the law by becoming a curse for us, for it is written: "Cursed is everyone who is hung on a pole." He redeemed us in order that the blessing given to Abraham might come to the Gentiles through Christ Jesus, so that by faith we might receive the promise of the Spirit (Galatians 3:13-14).

The New Covenant could not be inaugurated until the curse of the Old Covenant was removed. On the cross Jesus took on himself the curse of the Law. As Paul writes in another place, "*God made him who had no sin* **to be sin** *for us*, so that in him we might become the righteousness of God" (2 Corinthians 5:21). God took our sins and placed them on the sinless Christ, who died in our place. As a result, the Lord now gives the righteousness of Christ to whoever puts their trust in him. This is the meaning of justification.

There also remained the question of *payment* for the sins of Old Testament believers. As we have seen, previous to Christ's coming, God in his grace did offer acceptance and forgiveness to people on the basis of their faith. But no adequate payment had ever been made for those sins. Animal sacrifices were only a temporary provision of the Old Covenant and had only symbolic value in and of themselves, because "*it is* **impossible** *for the blood of bulls and goats to take away sins*" (Hebrews 10:4). These animal sacrifices could "cover" sins for a time (the meaning of *atonement*), but they could not "take them away." This shows the great importance of the identification of Jesus made by John the Baptist: "Look, the Lamb of God, who *takes away* the sin of the world!" (John 1:29).

So along with the removal of the curse of the Law, there also had to be a provision to pay for the sins of all those people from the Old Testament period before Christ came. Paul writes that one reason for Christ's death is to prove God's righteousness regarding his forgiveness of those Old Testament believers: "He did this to demonstrate his righteousness, because in his forbearance he had left the sins committed beforehand unpunished" (Romans 3:25).

Therefore, having settled these issues to close the book on the Old Covenant, the Lord was free to move forward with his eternal plan:

> *Christ is the mediator of a new covenant, that those who are called may receive the promised eternal inheritance—now that he has died as a ransom to set them free from the sins committed under the first covenant* (Hebrews 9:15).

So Jesus' death on the cross brought the Old Covenant to an end, and at the same time officially inaugurated the New Covenant.

The Cross, the Center of History

Have you ever gotten lost at a mall while trying to find a certain store? If so, you probably look for a display of the mall's layout. After locating your store on the map, you know how to get there...that is, assuming you know where you are right now. That's why on those maps they typically have a prominent arrow labeled *You are HERE*. Finally, you are equipped to find your way to your desired destination.

History is the same way. The Scriptures give us God's plan of history from the creation of all things in Genesis 1 all the way to the installation of his eternal kingdom in Revelation 22. As we have already seen, the Bible seems contradictory when we compare what it says in one place to what it says in another. For us to see that there is no contradiction and properly interpret what does and does not apply directly to us, we need a marker like that one on the map at the mall. We need a pointer saying, *You are HERE*.

Now, please hear me clearly: The entire Bible is the Word of God. That is not in question. But what *is* in question is *what directly applies to whom* in any given passage. When you are reading and interpreting the Scriptures, it is vitally important to know where you are in God's plan. Let's look at some examples of what I mean.

- When you read the book of Isaiah, written in the eighth century BC, you are reading God's Word as delivered to the people Israel under the Old Covenant.

- When you read Paul's letter to the Romans, written about AD 56, you are reading God's Word as delivered to Christians (both Jews and Gentiles) under the New Covenant.

- When you are reading Jesus' words to the man who is commonly referred to as the Rich Young Ruler in Luke 18:18-27, you are reading God's Word as delivered to...whom, and when? While this may be new to you, you are reading the record of God's Word through Jesus Christ to the people of Israel under the Old Covenant. Yes, I know the Gospel of Luke is found in what we call the "New Testament" portion of your Bible, but the events described took place under the Old Covenant, and must be interpreted accordingly.

The True Dividing Line

Historically, where are we now? What year is it anyway? That seems like such a simple question, one any schoolchild could answer. As I begin this manuscript, it's 2011. But according to whom? Who says so?

In world history there have been many ways of reckoning years. There was no established universal dating system until the middle of the sixth century, when the pope asked a Scythian monk named Dionysius Exiguus ("the Humble") to calculate the years and harmonize the various existing calendars. One scholar, tongue in cheek, suggests that his name should be translated "Dennis the Insignificant." Even if so, his impact on the world was anything but insignificant. It has been tweaked several times over the centuries, but by and large, the dating scheme created by Dionysius can still be seen in media the world over every day.

Dionysius' innovation was to calculate the years from the birth of Jesus, which he decided was year 753 of the Roman calendar. He named it AD 1. We now know he missed slightly and that Jesus was actually born somewhere in the years we call 6 to 4 BC, but he was remarkably accurate given the tools he had to work with. The birth of Christ became the dividing line of history, with the years before then counted as BC ("Before Christ"), and the years after called AD (*Anno Domini*, Latin for "the Year of our Lord").

But Dionysius did make a major mistake, in my opinion—one which has carried down to this very day, affecting the way non-Christians and Christians alike think about history. Much of the world today divides history according the *birth* of Jesus Christ. God, however, divides history according to the *death* of Jesus Christ.

While we can't be certain in what year Jesus died, AD 30 is a likely guess. This book was scheduled for publication in 2013. That means that, if we divided history the way God does, it would actually be in the year 1983. Our calendars are off by about 30 years. But this isn't just a controversy about numbers. It has huge ramifications for our interpretation of the Bible.

When Jesus was growing up, and then conducting his earthly

ministry, what covenant was in effect? If we are still in doubt, Paul tells us:

> When the set time had fully come, God sent his Son, born of a woman, *born under the law*, to redeem those under the law, that we might receive adoption to sonship (Galatians 4:4-5).

This means Jesus was born, grew up, conducted his public ministry, and died as a faithful Israelite living under the Old Covenant!

Looking at Jesus' Teaching in Historical Context

"Are you saying that the words of Jesus don't apply to me?" James nearly shouted into the phone. He was only one of scores of *People to People* listeners who have called and asked the same basic question. Many seemed fit to be tied.

From years of experience I can testify that few issues get people more upset than this one. I don't really blame them, especially those who are hearing it for the first time. After all, Jesus is our Savior, the Son of God who loved us and gave his life for us. A personal relationship with him is the heart of our faith, a fact that separates us from every religion of the world. Faithful Jews don't have a personal relationship with Moses. Faithful Muslims don't have a personal relationship with Mohammed. Neither do Buddhists with Buddha, or Confucians with Confucius.

Besides that, Jesus' teaching is widely acknowledged, even by non-believers and atheists, as the most advanced and wisest moral teaching in the history of the world. In many of our Bibles, his words are printed in red, which is a testimony to the reverence Christians have for him. We haven't seen Jesus with our eyes or heard his voice with our ears, but we have his words in red in our Bibles. *And now they're being taken away from us!* That's why people hit the ceiling.

So let me speak directly and clearly. I am not taking Jesus' words away from anyone. I am not saying you should not read them and love them. And I am not saying that you shouldn't apply them and live them out—*assuming you have done the work of accurately interpreting them in their historical context.* If Jesus lived and taught under the Old Covenant, which we have clearly established, then his words must be interpreted in light of that fact *before* you try to apply them in today's context.

The Example of the Sermon on the Mount

I want to take a key example from Jesus' teaching and use it to follow the same train of thought I would use on the air to answer someone like James: the Sermon on the Mount.

Few sayings in the history of the world are better known or more loved than those found in the Sermon on the Mount, which is found in Matthew chapters 5–7. And its context is all-important. What was going on at the time?

John the Baptist had begun preaching, "Repent, for the kingdom of heaven has come near" (Matthew 3:2). What would an average Jew have "heard" in this proclamation? He or she would have jumped in excitement. God was about to fulfill his promises. "Get ready," John was saying. "Repent, turn around and be faithful to the Old Covenant. The Lord offers forgiveness to those who do. The curse can be removed. He will soon send his kingdom to those who are faithful in Israel, but judgment to those who remain unrepentant."

After many centuries of oppression, revolutions, wars, and foreign domination, the phrase "the kingdom" had taken on a narrow meaning for Jews of the first century. For the average person it carried a primarily political meaning. The kingdom would come when God sent his messiah, a national leader, a freedom fighter—sort of a Jewish George Washington. He would lead Judea into a national war of independence, defeating and ejecting the hated Romans, and set himself up as God's king, the promised son of David.

Therefore, when Jesus took up the message, "Repent, for the kingdom of heaven has come near" (Matthew 4:17), he had the practical problem of correcting all the misconceptions attached to it and redefining them according to the truth. Most important, always knowing he was moving toward the cross, he had to prepare people to receive that message of salvation by grace through faith in him.

The Sermon on the Mount shows the Lord teaching to accomplish these very purposes. On one level it frustrated and confused the common person's expectations of the meaning of the kingdom. On another, it refocused their attention on the Law of Moses, casting it in a bright spotlight that showed its real meaning in unmistakable terms.

Early in the message Jesus issues the key point:

> I tell you that unless your righteousness surpasses that of the Pharisees and the teachers of the law, you will certainly not enter the kingdom of heaven (Matthew 5:20).

If that wasn't enough to drop everyone's jaws, Jesus goes on to explain. It is not enough to refrain from murder, he says—you must not be angry with your brother *in your heart*. It is not enough to refrain from adultery—you must not lust *in your heart*. He goes on to say that you must keep your marriage vows and not take any "easy" ways out, even if they're legal. You must not take revenge on others, and you must even love your enemies! Finally, to sum up what it means for your righteousness to surpass that of the Pharisees and teachers of the laws, he says,

> Be perfect, therefore, as your heavenly Father is perfect (5:48).

If we truly and deeply love Jesus' red-letter words, we have to ask, "What is their meaning? What did Jesus intend by them?" I believe that if you read them in the context of the time, the answer is clear: Jesus is focusing on the Law—but far beyond its literal surface meaning. He is drawing out the spirit of the Law. And keep in mind the comment that kicked off this section: Unless your righteousness is better than the best religious performers of the time, the Pharisees and teachers of the Law, "you will certainly not enter the kingdom of heaven."

Only Perfection Is Acceptable

So the Sermon on the Mount poses and answers the most important question in the world: "How good do I have to be in order to enter the kingdom of God?" Answer: You must "be *perfect*"! How "perfect"? You must be as perfect "as your heavenly Father is perfect"! It is the ultimate expression of the meaning of God's Law.

Jesus' sayings in the Sermon on the Mount have become almost institutionalized. You can see them done in calligraphy in nicely framed editions. You can find them artistically rendered in needlepoint and embroidery. You can find them displayed on thousands of beautifully designed websites. They are among the most well-known Bible verses, even among the public at large. But these sentimental responses to the sermon are utterly different from the way these words fell on their original listeners. The common audience of Jesus' time would have been disappointed, baffled, and deeply disturbed by this sermon. C.S. Lewis once compared it to "being knocked flat on [the] face by a sledge-hammer."

Jesus' mission was to die on the cross to provide salvation for the world. But before we are ready to trust in a Savior, we must know that we *need* a Savior. This is the teaching mission of the Old Covenant. As Paul writes,

> The law was our guardian until Christ came that we might
> be justified by faith. Now that this faith has come, we are
> no longer under a guardian (Galatians 3:24-25).

The Sermon on the Mount is the ultimate example of the meaning of God's Law, clearly showing that the only standard God will ever accept is unblemished *perfection*. Jesus delivered this sermon to a nation that watered down that standard and had become fixated on receiving their political deliverance. It was intended to create shock and awe. To anyone who carefully listens to its message even today, the effect is the same.

There is one more question I have come to expect from someone like James. In his case, he put it this way: "Wait a minute! Didn't Jesus say he didn't come to abolish the Law? So we still have to keep it!"

"You are exactly right, in part," I answered him. "Let's look at what he actually said." I then referred him back to the Scriptures:

> Do not think that I have come to abolish the Law or the Prophets; I have not come to abolish them but to fulfill them. For truly I tell you, until heaven and earth disappear, not the smallest letter, not the least stroke of a pen, will by any means disappear from the Law until everything is accomplished (Matthew 5:17-18).

"Yes," I continued. "Jesus did not come to *abolish* the Law. He didn't come to deny it or destroy it. But look at what he said he would do. He came to *fulfill* the Law and the Prophets. That means he came to accomplish them and bring them to completion." He accomplished for us completely what we could not do for ourselves.

The apostle Paul explains it this way:

> Christ is the culmination of the law so that there may be righteousness for everyone who *believes* (Romans 10:4).

Because Jesus' life and ministry up to the cross took place under the Old Covenant, they must be interpreted in that light. Yes, sometimes his words anticipate the New Covenant, such as his teaching on the Holy Spirit, who would come after his death and resurrection. However, the critical questions to ask when you are reading any passage of Scripture are, "Who said it to whom?" and "Under what covenant was it said?" Then you are prepared to find its intended meaning and can go on to find its proper application in your life today.

As Christians living under the New Covenant we can look at Jesus' words through different eyes. We are not people under the Old Covenant hearing an exposition of the Law, which demands perfect performance to avoid its curse. We approach Jesus' teaching as believers who are already accepted by God and indwelt by the Holy Spirit. Jesus' words may teach God's will for our attitudes and actions, but God's acceptance is no longer tied to them. Christ now lives in us and empowers us to do his will.

We have worked our way through the fulfillment of the Old Covenant at the cross and the simultaneous inauguration of the
New Covenant. In the chapters ahead, we will take a magnified look
at the promises and blessings Christ has purchased for us as our New
Covenant inheritance.

7

A New Heart

God's Answer for Dead People

I will put my law in their minds and write it on their hearts.
JEREMIAH 31:33

I have found few experiences more meaningful and exciting than the occasions I've been able to tour Israel. While the highlights are walking where Jesus walked and seeing so many actual places where biblical events occurred, I've also really enjoyed getting to know many Israelis, some of whom served as our guides, drivers, and hosts.

One man who made a major impression on me was a guide named Yosi. Yosi was a passionate, patriotic Israeli. He had served in the army during several significant military events, and he always spoke fervently about his commitment to his people and land. But something that set him apart was his biblical knowledge. I don't mean just what we would call the Old Testament. Yosi had read the New Testament hundreds of times by his estimate, and knew it better than almost any Christian he met.

There was just one problem. He didn't "get it." The New Testament message must be spiritually discerned—and if the person reading it does not have the Spirit of God in them, they will lean on their own understanding (see Proverbs 3:5-6). Yosi knew to an impressive level what it said, but he did not believe in Jesus Christ. We would be at a site along the shore of the Sea of Galilee, for example. As we discussed the story that occurred there, Yosi and I would sometimes stop, share, and compare the accounts of the Bible at different locations.

I finally had the opportunity to have an extended conversation with him one-on-one, and it was very enjoyable. The flow of talk made it appropriate for me to probe him a little, and he was open to it. I opened up the Bible and showed him a passage from the Law of Moses that prophesies of the New Covenant:

> The LORD your God will circumcise your hearts and the hearts of your descendants, so that you may love him with all your heart and with all your soul, and live (Deuteronomy 30:6).

"What does that mean to you, Yosi?" I asked him. "What does this mean about circumcising your hearts?"

Yosi shrugged his shoulders and threw up his hands in despair. "I don't know!" he said.

What a striking contrast! Detailed and thorough knowledge on the one hand, and the inability to see the application and the connections to God's overall plan on the other.

Yosi represents to me a vivid picture of unbelieving Israel through the centuries. No nation ever loved and pored over their holy scriptures more than Israel. But no nation ever so badly missed the meaning of them, either. It shows why God must take the initiative and work in the hearts of people before the New Covenant will ever take root and grow in believing hearts.

Humanity's Need Beyond Forgiveness

If you ask average Christians what it means to be "saved," they will usually tell you something along these lines: "Salvation means that Jesus died for my sins so I can go to heaven when I die." But that's only the tip of the iceberg. Before Christ came into my life I needed forgiveness, certainly, but my need went much deeper. This is true for me, for Yosi, for you, for all of us. Our deeper problem is *what we are* as a result of sin. Forgiveness can change our status before a holy God, but it does not change our nature or give enlightenment to our spiritual understanding. No matter what we do on the outside, we cannot change our nature.

The problem of fallen humanity is not just that we are sinners in need of forgiveness (though that is certainly true!); we are also spiritually *dead* and in need of *life—God's life*. Only the resurrected Christ can give this life—his eternal life living in us is our only hope of glory. Through our efforts to live up to the law, we can improve, reform, change our external appearance and behavior, yes—*but we cannot change our natures*. We need God to do for us what we cannot do for ourselves. Therefore he said through Jeremiah, "I will put my law in their minds and write it on their hearts" (Jeremiah 31:33). This is one of the great promises of the New Covenant: God will do his work *within us*, changing our hearts and natures and leading and empowering us from the inside out.

The teaching function of the Law is to make us aware of our need. While only Israel was actually "under the Law," it continues to function in the same way it always did for anyone who looks into it. As I pointed out previously, the Law first teaches us about God's holiness, character, and standards, and then works like a mirror to reflect back to us our hopeless condition and need for a Savior. Paul wrote,

> We know that whatever the law says, it says to those who are under the law, so that every mouth may be silenced and the whole world held accountable to God. Therefore no one will be declared righteous in God's sight by the works of the law; rather, *through the law we become conscious of our sin* (Romans 3:19-20).

The first level of understanding for most of us is the discovery that we have thought thoughts and committed sinful actions against the holiness of God. Normal people have some sense of guilt—vague and generalized though it may be—for things they have done to others, such as lying, stealing, cheating, and harming others emotionally or physically. Even non-Christians on the street are apt to admit, "Well, I know I'm not perfect."

But those who continue to follow and give honest effort to living up to what the Scriptures teach will discover the next level of spiritual self-awareness. You become aware that your problem is much greater than some bad things you've done. You find that God looks upon the heart and your real problem is the ugliness that bubbles up from the depths of your heart. When this knowledge comes home to you, it can hit you like a load of bricks, and you cry out, "There's something really wrong with me!" Yes, you still want to know you are forgiven from what you've *done*, but this goes much deeper. You begin to long for deliverance from what you *are*.

This is about shame of the deepest and real kind, not false shame based on misunderstanding or unbiblical training. This is the real thing—being ashamed both of what you've done, and of what you *are*. The realization of what it means to "fall short of the glory of God" (Romans 3:23) hits you like a load of bricks. You are coming to understand for real how much you need a Savior!

Rescue from What We Are

The apostle Paul knew this experience and wrote about it. Having read this passage with thousands of people, I can tell you that there is almost 100 percent identification with these words:

> We know that the law is spiritual; but I am unspiritual, sold as a slave to sin. I do not understand what I do. For what I want to do I do not do, but what I hate I do...I know that good itself does not dwell in me, that is, in my sinful nature. For I have the desire to do what is good, but I cannot carry it out. For I do not do the good I want to do, but the evil I do not want to do—this I keep on doing (Romans 7:14-19).

I remember sharing this paragraph with a radio listener named Luke, and he half-seriously exclaimed, "Have you been spying on me?" I laughed and replied, "That's pretty much how everybody feels who hears this passage." I went on to comment, "You know, Luke, the encouraging part is that this is the apostle Paul speaking. Not a bad Christian! In other words, we're in good company. But the sad part is that this is the experience of anyone who sincerely tries to be 'good enough' for God." I then read what Paul said next:

> So I find this law at work: Although I want to do good, evil is right there with me. For in my inner being I delight in God's law; but I see another law at work in me, waging war against the law of my mind and making me a prisoner of the law of sin at work within me. What a wretched man I am! Who will rescue me from this body that is subject to death? (Romans 7:21-24).

For about 2000 years now, Christians have struggled to work out the principles of law and grace. Multitudes, it seems, have tried to enjoy the gospel of grace while still hanging onto law. But the principles are totally incompatible. Paul's cry, "What a wretched man I am! Who will rescue me free from this body that is subject to death?" is as far as the Law can take you. If you exert your best efforts to live up to it, it will bring you here and drop you. The Old Covenant has no answer for Paul's agonized question.

But Paul's next line is, "Thanks be to God, who delivers me through Jesus Christ our Lord!" (Romans 7:25). Only in the New Covenant is there a complete answer to the need of humanity. That's why the issue of our heart problem can be summed up in these verses:

> *What the law was powerless to do* in that it was weakened by the flesh, *God did* by sending his own Son in the likeness of sinful flesh to be a sin offering. And so he condemned sin in the flesh, in order that the righteous requirement of the law might be fully met in us, who do not live according to the flesh but according to the Spirit (Romans 8:3-4).

I believe the whole issue of the Old and New Covenants can be summed up in two phrases from this passage: "What the law was powerless to do…God did"! Why was the Law "powerless"? Because it depended on fallen human beings to keep it, which never happened and never will. Therefore God did for us what we could not accomplish on our own. He sent Jesus Christ to die on the cross to deal with the problem of our guilt before a holy God; then having raised him from the dead and us along with him, he gave us his Holy Spirit to indwell us, lead us from within, transform us, and empower us as we trust him— fulfilling his New Covenant promise: "I will put my law in their minds and write it on their hearts."

This promise is the greatest news in the world to those of us who have come to a real understanding of our need. We find fulfillment in Christ who says "I AM" the Living Water, the daily Bread, the good Shepherd. But there have always been many who think they're basically "good enough" and see little need for God to do a work within them.

The Man Who Thought He Was Good Enough

Nervous, excited, afraid of being seen, one of Israel's most respected rabbis and national leaders sought out Jesus after dark. He wasn't exactly sure who Jesus was or what his significance might be, but there was no denying that something supernatural surrounded him. The man's name was Nicodemus. He wanted to communicate that he was open and interested in Jesus, but unsure beyond that. "Rabbi," he said, "we know that you are a teacher who has come from God. For no one could perform the signs you are doing if God were not with him" (John 3:2). Nicodemus thought he was being complimentary. He was totally unprepared for what came next:

> Jesus replied, "Very truly I tell you, no one can see the kingdom of God unless they are born again" (John 3:3).

What a thing to say to a man who is a believer in the God of Israel and a revered teacher! Nicodemus's first reaction was frankly surprise. He was taken aback. It's hard to know from the text whether he was honestly baffled or slightly irritated: "How can someone be born when they are old?…Surely they cannot enter a second time into their mother's womb to be born!" (verse 4).

Moving past the man's reply, Jesus goes on to expand on his answer, adding a number of hints:

> "Very truly I tell you, no one can enter the kingdom of God unless they are born of water and the Spirit. Flesh gives birth to flesh, but the Spirit gives birth to spirit. You should not be surprised at my saying, 'You must be born again.' The wind blows wherever it pleases. You hear its sound, but you cannot tell where it comes from or where it is going. So it is with everyone born of the Spirit" (verses 5-8).

Once again, Nicodemus seems clueless. "How can this be?" he asks (verse 9). This time, Jesus seems taken aback. He appears incredulous at Nicodemus' confusion:

> "You are Israel's teacher," said Jesus, "and do you not understand these things?" (verse 10).

The Lord clearly expected that someone known and respected as "Israel's teacher" should easily understand what he was alluding to. It is all there in the Law and the Prophets. Jesus' words to Nicodemus echo several prophecies of the New Covenant, ones any Old Testament scholar should know like the back of his hand.

Nicodemus had dedicated his life and career to studying and living by the Law. He had gained prominence and earned the esteem of his nation because of his performance. If there was a note of irritation in his replies, this is probably why. By all normal external standards of his culture and time, he was already a good man and was considered one of the great teachers of the Law. He may have approached Jesus hoping to be accepted as a peer and enjoy a stimulating rabbi-to-rabbi discussion. But what he certainly did not expect was the suggestion that there was something wrong with him, that he needed something more! Jesus was saying he needed an entirely new quality of life that comes from God alone. God's Spirit invades a human life, and now there can be a living, personal relationship—Spirit-to-spirit communication.

Ezekiel's Prophecy of the New Covenant

Jesus' second comment to Nicodemus, about being "born of water and the Spirit," has generated much controversy through the centuries. "The Spirit" is obviously a reference to the Holy Spirit, but what is the "water"? Some have suggested that it refers to water baptism. Some say it's a symbol for repentance. Others believe it's a reference to physical birth. For the record, I believe the reference is obvious. Jesus is pointing his fellow rabbi back to one of the most prominent prophecies of the New Covenant given through Ezekiel, a contemporary of Jeremiah, in which God said,

> I will sprinkle clean **water** on you, and you will be clean; I will cleanse you from all your impurities and from all your idols. I will give you **a new heart** and put a **new spirit** in you; I will remove from you your heart of stone and give you a **heart of flesh**. And I will put **my Spirit** in you and move you to follow my decrees and be careful to keep my laws. Then you will live in the land I gave your ancestors; you will be my people, and I will be your God (Ezekiel 36:25-28).

By this time in our journey you probably notice many similarities between Ezekiel's prophecy and Jeremiah's. The promises given here by God are all *unilateral* and *unconditional*, for one. The prophecy also echoes Jeremiah's in the phrase "you will be my people, and I will be your God." Then, compare Ezekiel's words to where the Lord said through Jeremiah, "I will forgive their wickedness and will remember their sins no more." The promise to deal with his people's sins is expanded here, and described using the image of washing with "water." Finally, God's promise to "put my law in their minds and write it on their hearts" is richly elaborated upon. The Lord says he will replace their "heart of stone" with a "new heart," a "heart of flesh." God will put his own Spirit within his people and empower them intrinsically to live according to his will.

I believe Jesus' words about being "born of the water and the Spirit" are a clear reference to this passage. He is saying in so many words, "Nicodemus, the New Covenant is here! I AM the New Covenant—I will usher in that which was promised in the past." This also explains his surprise that Nicodemus didn't get it: "You are Israel's teacher, and do you not understand these things?" Jesus clearly expects that any knowledgeable Old Testament scholar would have caught his allusion immediately.

Additional evidence that this is the passage Jesus has in mind is his comparison of the Spirit to the "wind" that "blows wherever it pleases." In Ezekiel 37, immediately after the passage above, we find the striking vision of the valley of bones. God shows Ezekiel this vision, then commands him to call the bones to life. A rushing wind (or "breath") comes, and the jumbled skeletons come back together, stand up, and are covered with flesh, now living human beings. As the Lord explains to the prophet, this is a vivid picture of the restoration and spiritual resurrection of Israel in the New Covenant. In both Hebrew and Greek, one single word means both "wind," "breath," and "spirit." That's why "wind" and "breath" are often biblical symbols of the Holy Spirit. So the reference to "wind" by Jesus is also a hint that points back to Ezekiel's New Covenant prophecies. The wind represents the Spirit of God giving life to the dead.

Our Need for Life

God's promise of life to the dead is not primarily a reference to the future resurrection of the body, though salvation certainly includes that. It is a reference to the *restoration of spiritual life to fallen human beings*. Why do people need spiritual life? The simple and obvious answer is because, apart from Jesus Christ, we are spiritually *dead*. In the 25 years I have spoken with listeners on live radio, I believe this is the insight that has grabbed more believers and changed more lives than any other.

Max was a typical example. "I've been a Christian since I was a child, probably since six or seven years old," he explained. "I've always been taught that my sins are forgiven because Jesus died on the cross for me. I've never seriously doubted that I'm a child of God and that I'll go to heaven when I die. But I don't understand what you're saying when you say that salvation is more than forgiveness of sins."

"Max, I totally understand where you're coming from," I said. "In fact, that's pretty much what I would have said during the first ten years after I became a Christian. I won't minimize in any way how wonderful it is to know your sins are forgiven, but salvation is more than that. Our minds need to be renewed by the Word of God. We need to be changed and empowered to live on a whole new level if we're going to be the kind of people the Lord wants us to be."

I went on to briefly tell my story of driving down the freeway with tears streaming down my cheeks, busy and barren in my work in the ministry. It was coming to the end of my own resources trying to live the Christian life that opened me up to become teachable and learn what I had not seen before. I then opened the Bible and shared several passages with Max to help him grasp what this issue of spiritual life and death are all about, the same passages that had led me down the path of understanding.

Jesus said, "I have come that they may have *life*, and have it to the full" (John 10:10). I remembered hearing Major Ian Thomas teach, and how he repeatedly spoke of "the *living* Christ" and "Christ *living in me*." I had read the verse in John 10 many times, but now it jumped out at me. *What kind of people need "life"?* I pondered. *Only **dead** people need "life."* But who fits in that category?

Once on the trail, I found what Paul wrote:

> As for you, *you were **dead** in your transgressions and sins*, in which you used to live when you followed the ways of this world and of the ruler of the kingdom of the air, the spirit who is now at work in those who are disobedient. All of us also lived among them at one time, gratifying the cravings of *our flesh* and following its desires and thoughts. Like the rest *we were **by nature** deserving of wrath* (Ephesians 2:1-3).

Our Hopeless State Before Christ

If you had asked me before what the problem of man is outside of Christ, I would have said, like most people, "We are guilty sinners in need of forgiveness." That is true, of course, but this passage goes far beyond that. It says that in the eyes of God we are dead in our natural states, and our very natures are corrupted. When we sin, we are simply doing what comes naturally, and there is no human remedy for these problems. No matter what we try or how hard we try it, we cannot change what we are. And beyond that, even worse, *no dead person can raise himself or herself from the dead.*

In his amazing mercy and grace, the Lord has provided a complete salvation for us! Paul continues in Ephesians 2,

> But because of his great love for us, God, who is rich in mercy, *made us alive with Christ* even when we were *dead* in transgressions—it is by grace you have been saved (verses 4-5).

Once you accept this teaching of the New Testament, it seems you begin to see it everywhere. Continuing to read, I found this passage:

> When *you were dead* in your transgressions and in the uncircumcision of your flesh, *God made you alive with Christ.* He forgave us all our sins, having canceled the charge of our legal indebtedness, which stood against us and condemned us; he has taken it away, nailing it to the cross (Colossians 2:13-14).

The apostle Paul packs an incredible amount of truth into these verses:

1. We see again that our original state is one of spiritual death, but that God has made us alive with Christ.

2. There is a reference to our fallen nature, which he describes as being in a state of "uncircumcision," a problem also solved through our new life in Christ.

3. It says that God will provide total forgiveness for "all our sins"—past, present, and future—something never available under the Law.

4. There is the clear declaration that the Law—the "written code, with its regulations, that was against us and stood opposed to us"—has been decisively fulfilled for us by Christ Jesus. As a result there is nothing left for you and me to fulfill. Rather, we can rest in what God has done because of his love for us. The Old Covenant officially ended when Christ died, and is described as being nailed to the cross. The New Covenant reigns!

Once you see how terrible our state is outside of Christ, you never again question why the Law could provide no solution to our need. The Old Covenant has no answer for these problems. Only Christ is the answer, and the remedies come only through the New Covenant.

Fallen men and women need more than forgiveness, more than teaching, more than the standard motivations of reward and punishment, more than religious functions and actions. We need to be *restored to spiritual life* and *remade* before we can once again become truly functional from the perspective of our Creator. Christ sets us free to be real—not actors and hypocrites.

Power to Believe and Love

In the New Covenant promise, the Lord says he will write his law in our minds and on our hearts. A common question I hear is "Which law?" Does that refer to the Ten Commandments? Is it talking about the Law of Moses?

No, neither of those is the answer. The "law" God refers to is the law of love which we apply to every situation—just as Jesus loved and so fulfilled the Law. This law means in general terms "doing his will from the heart." This is foreshadowed by David's assertion in Psalm 40, which was fulfilled by Jesus Christ according to Hebrews 10:5-7. David said, "I desire to do your will, my God; your law is within my heart"

(Psalm 40:8). Jesus was the only one in history who lived out this principle perfectly. As he himself said,

> I have come down from heaven not to do my will but to do the will of him who sent me (John 6:38).

Jesus ultimately fulfilled his commitment to do the Father's will in going to the cross on our behalf. The night before his death, with his humanity agonizing over the horror of the cross, he remained faithful:

> "*Abba*, Father," he said, "everything is possible for you. Take this cup from me. Yet not what I will, but what you will" (Mark 14:36).

God's purpose is to redeem and recreate millions of children who will also live according to his will from the heart. And what does that look like? The Lord has told us:

- *To believe in Christ.* When Jesus was asked what people needed to do "to do the will of God," he answered, "The work of God is this: to believe in the one he has sent" (John 6:29). Believing, of course, is not a one-time event at the moment of salvation. To become a "believer" is to get on a path of learning to trust him and rely upon him in every area of life.

- *To love one another.* Jesus said, "A new command I give you: Love one another. As I have loved you, so you must love one another. By this everyone will know that you are my disciples, if you love one another" (John 13:34-35).

The apostle John summed up the will of God—that is, what it means to "keep his commandments," this way:

> This is his command: to believe in the name of his Son, Jesus Christ, and to love one another as he commanded us (1 John 3:23).

To believe and to love sound so simple! And yet, for anyone who sincerely tries to do so, we find that this is beyond our unaided ability. We need God to continue to work in our hearts and supply his power to live out his will. This he promises to do under the New Covenant.

The Coming of the Holy Spirit

John the Baptist was the final prophet of the Old Covenant. As Jesus said, "All the Prophets and the Law prophesied until John" (Matthew 11:13). But he was also the first voice of the coming kingdom and the forerunner of the Messiah.

John's appearance as the first prophet sent to Israel in 400 years stirred up considerable excitement, and many wondered if he were the Messiah. No, he always said, his message was to announce the coming of someone greater:

> After me comes one more powerful than I, the straps of whose sandals I am not worthy to stoop down and untie. I baptize you with water, but *he will baptize you with the Holy Spirit* (Mark 1:7-8).

This was one of the most important provisions of the promised New Covenant: the giving of God's Holy Spirit to human beings. Isaiah, Ezekiel, Joel, and others prophesied this. Now John appeared, saying the greater one to follow would fulfill it. John's words were a clear New Covenant signal to anyone who knew the Scriptures.

The last night before he went to the cross for us, Jesus spoke at length to his disciples about the Holy Spirit. He said,

> I will ask the Father, and he will give you another *advocate* to help you and be with you forever—the *Spirit of truth*. The world cannot accept him, because it neither sees him nor knows him. But you know him, for he lives with you and *will be in you* (John 14:16-17).

The word translated "advocate" here can also mean "helper," "counselor," or "encourager." He will come to be "in you," Jesus said. He goes on to explain that by means of the Holy Spirit, Christ himself and the Father will be in them:

> I will not leave you as orphans; I will come to you. Before long, the world will not see me anymore, but you will see me. *Because I live, you also will live.* On that day you will realize that I am in my Father, and you are in me, and *I am in you*...Anyone who loves me will obey my teaching. My Father will love them, and *we* will come to them and *make our home with them* (John 14:18-20,23).

God is a Trinity, or "Tri-unity": three Persons in one divine essence. He is not "three Gods" but one God. He cannot be divided. Therefore, if the Spirit is in us, Christ is in us. And if Christ is in us, the Father is in us. This is beyond our comprehension, but by faith we can take it as what God has clearly taught us in the Bible. The three Persons are often shown acting in different roles. For example, the Father sent the Son to become the Savior of the world. Then Jesus the Son, having risen from the dead and now exalted to the Father's right hand, together with the Father sends the Holy Spirit to whoever trusts in him.

On the day of Pentecost following Jesus' resurrection, the promise of the Holy Spirit was fulfilled (described in Acts 2), and the age of the New Covenant was fully launched. Since that time, possession of God's Holy Spirit has been the inheritance of every child of God, all those who put their faith in Jesus Christ.

The Work of the Spirit in God's Promise

As we close this chapter, let's summarize what the Holy Spirit has come to do in his ministry to fulfill God's great promise, "I will put my law in their minds and write it on their hearts."

- *The Holy Spirit regenerates (gives life to) those who trust in Christ.* We have seen that fallen human beings are spiritually *dead*, and the only solution to death is *life*. Whenever someone hears the gospel and believes the good news, the

Holy Spirit restores spiritual life to that person: "Because of his great love for us, God, who is rich in mercy, made us alive with Christ" (Ephesians 2:4-5).

- *The Holy Spirit baptizes us into Christ.* As we have seen, we are all born into this world "in Adam." How can that be changed? In simple terms, by doing away with the "old self" and raising up a "new self" in Christ. That's what water baptism signifies: the work of the Holy Spirit. He unites us with Christ in his death, which does away with our old identity in Adam, then he raises us up as someone brand-new: "We were therefore buried with him through baptism into death in order that, just as Christ was raised from the dead through the glory of the Father, we too may live a new life" (Romans 6:4). The clear contrast is seen in 1 Corinthians 15:22: "For as *in Adam all die,* so *in Christ all will be made alive.*"

- *The Holy Spirit permanently indwells believers.* Having received new life in Christ, we now have the Holy Spirit living inside us. This is why we can say, "Jesus Christ lives in me," and this is how God empowers New Covenant believers to live—by listening to his Spirit. Though not all believers have been taught much about the Holy Spirit or about his ministry in their lives, he lives in every believer without exception: "You, however, are not in the realm of the flesh but are in the realm of the Spirit, if indeed the Spirit of God lives in you. And *if anyone does not have the Spirit of Christ, they do not belong to Christ*" (Romans 8:9).

Paul had all this in mind when he wrote these powerful words:

Through the law *I died to the law so that I might live for God.* I have been crucified with Christ and I no longer live, but *Christ lives in me.* The life I now live in the body, *I live by faith in the Son of God,* who loved me and gave himself for me (Galatians 2:19-20).

There's much more to see regarding how the Lord intends us to live this new life, and I will explore that with you in later chapters. But this is the foundation. We could never on our own raise ourselves to life or change our natures, but God has done the work for us through his Holy Spirit. Because of his grace in Jesus Christ, we have new life, a new heart, a new nature, and powerful new resources to enable us to fulfill his will for us in this world. And his will is that we love one another.

8

Unconditional Acceptance

What God Has Always Wanted

I will be their God, and they will be my people.
JEREMIAH 31:33

Back in college I became a member of the Sigma Chi fraternity. On one level, fraternities and sororities appear strange and silly, especially to outsiders. Members are known by the Greek letters they wear on their shirts. Though the details are kept secret, it is known that they have an inner core of passwords, handshakes, and rituals, and members refer to each other as brothers or sisters.

It's not just something that attracts young men and women, either. Many members of fraternities and sororities stay active as long as they live, and consider their association to be extremely precious. I also have kept some of my fraternity brothers as lifelong friends.

Human beings have a deep inner drive to *belong*. I consider that to be evidence of man's spiritual nature and a genuine need, along with the needs for *identity*, *love and acceptance*, and *meaning and purpose*. We all want to know the answers to the questions, "Who am I?"; "Who will make me complete?"; "Why am I here?"

You see the drive for belonging throughout life. Kids want to be on sports, dance, or other kinds of teams or in organizations like the

Scouts or in their own little "clubs." In middle school, social cliques become all-important, determining who is "in" and who is "out." What do we mean by the term "peer pressure" but the irresistible drive for acceptance that influences people to do what they would not do otherwise? In many areas, gangs become the dominant way for young men or women to find out who they are, which leads to much misery and crime. Then for those who are privileged to attend college, fraternities, sororities, many other academic and service organizations, and informal groups provide vehicles for students to belong.

It doesn't end there, of course. In the adult world there are countless organizations, brotherhoods, sisterhoods, and group pursuits. Some of these are positive, some are negative, but all are attempts to meet the deep, undeniable inner need of human beings to be somebody, to belong, to look for approval. We have this need because God made us this way. It is a deep-seated longing for eternity—a longing that can only be filled by the Eternal One, the Holy Spirit.

Do you recall from the first chapter the letter written to me by Evelyn? She talked about her desperate and determined efforts to serve, which were finally rewarded by being given the key to the church. But after all that, she was still empty. What was she really looking for?

Have you ever wondered why God made us to begin with? Two of the most common answers people give are "to worship him" and "to serve him." Both of these are true to an extent, but they are only partial answers.

Yes, God desires us to worship him, because he is a God of truth, and he is worthy of all praise and worship. And he wants us to serve him, because it's the way we can enjoy participating in his plan in the world. But neither of these is why God created us. He always wanted something more. It's there in one of the promises of the New Covenant: "I will be their God, and they will be my people" (Jeremiah 31:33). He wanted us to be his children, to experience a deep love that cannot come from any other source.

God Made Us for Relationship

Let's use a human example. Amy and I have been blessed with two wonderful children, and now four grandchildren. Great-grandchildren may not be that far in our future. Why did we have kids to begin with?

We didn't have Debbie and Bob just so I could have two people to tell me how great I am and feed my ego. I have Amy for that. (The sound you just heard was Amy dissolving in laughter.)

We also didn't have our children so they would do chores. Now, we expected them to do some chores—doing dishes, cutting the grass, helping with laundry, picking up around the house as they grew up. No, we had children so we could *love them* and *be loved by them*—in other words, to enjoy a relationship.

That's why God made us. Because he wanted to enjoy a relationship with his unique creatures called human beings. He created us in his own image, with the capacity to know him, receive his love, and love him in return. While it is awesome and mind-boggling to ponder, the infinite, eternal, unlimited God actually *cares* whether or not little grains of sand like you and me know him and love him! Not because he needs us, but because "God is love" (1 John 4:8).

This is also the answer to another common question: "If God knew people were going to choose to sin, why did he give them free will?" While there are mysteries of his infiniteness and wisdom beyond my ability to understand, I think I can answer this to some extent. God had to give us free will because he wanted a genuine relationship based on love. If we had been created without the capacity of free choice, robot-like, we might have been *functionally* pleasing to God, as the inanimate creation and animals are. But we could never be *morally* pleasing to him, nor could you describe us as enjoying a genuine relationship with him. Apart from free will, we would have been mere machines.

That's why God "risked" giving man freedom, allowing humans to be unique, creative, responsive, blooming. There is always a risk in love, because it cannot be coerced from another. The other party must be free to love or not love, or it is not love at all. The opportunity to love or not love that was given to Adam and Eve was not a charade. It was a moment of genuine free choice, with tremendous consequences. I hedge a little by putting quotation marks around "risked," because we are talking about God here. Since he lives beyond time, there was never any question in his mind what they would do, but knowing it, he also always intended to send his Son to be the Savior his fallen creatures would need.

What God Has Always Wanted

God has always wanted a relationship with human beings. The entrance of sin into human experience created a vast gulf between him—the holy, living God—and sinful, spiritually dead people. But still, even in the midst of the fall and afterward, his desire did not change. This is consistent throughout the Bible. Adam and Eve "heard the sound of the LORD God as he was walking in the garden in the cool of the day" (Genesis 3:8). They hid from him in fear and shame, but the Lord called, "Where are you?" (verse 9). He cared, as he cares for us now. No matter how deep in trouble we have chosen to wallow, he is still pursuing, restoring, loving.

Later, we are told of one of the few faithful persons before the flood, Enoch, who "walked faithfully with God" (Genesis 5:24)—so much so that he was taken to heaven without dying. The writer of Hebrews comments,

> Before he was taken, *he was commended as one who pleased God. And without faith it is impossible to please God,* because anyone who comes to him must believe that he exists and that he rewards those who earnestly seek him (Hebrews 11:5-6).

The only way anyone in any age has been able to please God has been through *faith*. No one was ever able to earn God's acceptance through law-keeping, but people in the Old Testament period were able to live in a way pleasing to God by pursuing a relationship with him through faith. He has always been looking for people who come to him on the basis of truth, humility, and sincere faith—people who know they aren't worthy to stand before him and be accepted on their own merits, but who come trusting in his mercy, grace, and compassion. These, God says, are the ones who get his attention: "True worshipers will worship the Father in the Spirit and in truth, for they are the kind of worshipers the Father seeks" (John 4:23).

For those who got all tangled up in the complexities and requirements of the Old Covenant, the prophet Micah raised and answered
the fundamental question "What does God want?"

> With what shall I come before the LORD and bow down
> before the exalted God? Shall I come before him with burnt
> offerings, with calves a year old? Will the LORD be pleased
> with thousands of rams, with ten thousand rivers of oil? Shall
> I offer my firstborn for my transgression, the fruit of my body
> for the sin of my soul? (Micah 6:6-7).

Micah starts with the rhetorical question, "What do I have to do to
be okay with God?" He "raises the ante" with each phrase, progressing
from offering animal sacrifices to the hypothetical sacrifice of his own
child. You can almost hear his voice rising with each suggestion. But
then he provides the clear, straightforward answer:

> He has shown you, O mortal, what is good. And what does
> the LORD require of you? *To act justly and to love mercy and
> to **walk humbly with your God*** (verse 8).

Micah is saying in effect to the people of Israel, "You don't have to
leap over rushing rivers, climb mighty mountains, or swim across the
ocean to be acceptable and pleasing to God. All he asks for is people of
faith, who express it in loving their neighbors as themselves and walking humbly in relationship with him."

This relationship focus comes to reality in the New Testament,
when Jesus completed all that God wants on our behalf. We cannot
do it. We rest in the finished work of Christ—not in ourselves. In his
great prayer the night before his death, the Lord Jesus gives us the very
essence of real life here and now:

> This *is eternal life: **that they know you, the only true God,
> and Jesus Christ***, whom you have sent (John 17:3).

This is echoed by the apostle John in his first letter, one of the final
books of the New Testament to be written:

> We know…that the Son of God has come and has given us understanding, *so that we may know him who is true*. And we are in him who is true by being in his Son Jesus Christ. He is the true God and eternal life (1 John 5:20).

This is why God made us. He has not always dealt with the human race the same way throughout history, but behind that, from Genesis to Revelation, his desire has always been for a relationship with us.

The Lure of Legalism

We can know that the Lord always intended to make a New Covenant, because he knows the end from the beginning. The Old Covenant was not a surprise to him. He knew from the beginning that humanity in itself could not walk perfectly by being led outwardly by the Law. God is perfect and he demanded perfection. It's not as if he tried "Plan A," called "Law," and when it didn't work, he had to scramble and come up with "Plan B," called "Grace." No, he always intended to make this New Covenant, which is also called the "*eternal* covenant" (Hebrews 13:20). "If that's the case," people often ask, "why didn't God just start the New Covenant from the beginning? Why go through all this history and through an Old Covenant that would eventually fail?"

I am asked questions beginning with "*Why did God…?* " all the time. Unless the Bible specifically tells us, we are on shaky ground trying to speculate on why God does something, but sometimes we can make a "sanctified educated guess." Here's my best guess about why he has organized history the way he has. He has always worked with individuals all over the world in every era of history. But he has also worked, and still is working, with *the human race as a whole*. It appears to me that the Lord has given the human family the opportunity to explore life and attempt to live under every kind of condition.

Fallen man got to live according to his own devices and powers apart from divine Law in the centuries before Moses. The people of Israel got to try living under the Law during the time of the Old Covenant. Now, the gospel of Jesus Christ is proclaimed all over the world, and people who trust in him get the opportunity to live under the New Covenant. The New Covenant also gives opportunity to people to become new in Christ. "If anyone is in Christ, he is a new creation. The old has passed away; behold, the new has come" (2 Corinthians 5:17 ESV)

The Old Covenant did not fail. It accomplished what God wanted—that we could come to see ourselves as helpless, wretched, in need of a Savior. As we turn to Jesus by faith, he gives us a new heart so we can be led from within by the Holy Spirit.

One thing that will be consistently demonstrated throughout every age is that *human beings cannot live successfully as human beings apart from total dependence upon God.* It doesn't matter if we are left to our own devices, put under the yoke of God's Law, given the blessings of the New Covenant, or even governed by the Lord in person. Human performance will always end in failure if it does not flow from a love relationship with our Creator and if it is not empowered by the Lord himself. No human being will be able to say, "If only things had been different, I would have done better." The panorama of history will decisively squash that potential excuse.

Individually we often seem to reproduce the history of the human race on a smaller scale: We start out unbelieving and ignorant, living without God in our lives. Then we become aware of his reality but try living according to law or tradition, believing that *I can do this if I just try hard enough.* Typically, people aren't ready to receive the fullness of the grace of God until they have experienced sufficient personal failure. It seems most of us have to go through a "Romans 7 experience" (discovering that "what I want to do I do not do, but what I hate I do...What a wretched man I am!") before we are prepared to willingly receive an acceptance based on the sheer grace of God accomplished by Christ's finished work on the cross.

That certainly was my experience. As I have recounted, during the first years after I received Christ, I lived on the joy of his love and life and was fueled by the excitement of seeing him use me to draw others to him. But after going into full-time ministry, I began to accumulate more and more rules, expectations, and unconscious legalisms. As I described in chapter 3, I became more and more prideful, judgmental of others, and bogged down in the work of ministry. My joy drained away and I dried up, all while outwardly doing more and more things that were "impressive" in the eyes of others for the cause of Christ.

I later described my course this way: "I went into the ministry in order to change the world, but the world wasn't changed. Then I came to Dallas in order to change Dallas, but Dallas wasn't changed. Then I founded my new ministry to change the church, but the church wasn't changed. Finally, after a long period of joylessness, dryness, and ineffectiveness, I came to the realization: *I couldn't even change me!*"

That's when I was desperate and miserable enough to become totally teachable. And that's exactly when the Lord began to teach me about his love, grace, and acceptance on a completely new and fantastic scale.

Our Craving for Acceptance

Ashley called the radio program one night. She sounded deeply discouraged and sad. "Bob, I don't understand what's happened to me. I became a Christian four years ago, and it was so exciting at first. But I've totally lost it. Where did my joy go?"

I asked her to tell me more about her journey. Ashley said, "For a long time I was on a high because God loved me and forgave me for my sins. It was almost like a honeymoon period. I was so excited to start volunteering at church, and before long I was one of the supervisors in the children's Sunday-school department. There were great things going on.

"Our church had lots of really good programs. I tried to do everything our pastor said. I started his program to read the Bible all the way through in a year. I volunteered to help with Vacation Bible School. My husband used to complain that I was at church all the time, but what could I do? I wanted us to start tithing, but my husband didn't think we could. He also didn't want to go on Sunday nights or Wednesday nights, so I would go without him sometimes. Then, another lady at church started urging me to go on a mission trip with her to Russia. It sounded really exciting, but I have three children at home, and it made me nervous to think about leaving them to go overseas, but I went."

Ashley went on to list about six more projects and ministries she had taken on. I began to think she wouldn't stop talking long enough for me to get a word in edgewise, but she suddenly stopped. Then I could hear sounds of crying.

"Ashley," I said gently, "I am sure you are sincere in wanting to do all these things. But let me ask you this: *Why* are you doing all these things?"

"Because I want to please God," she said. "But I just can't. I'm so tired. I don't ever read my Bible anymore. My husband is mad at me and tired of God. I don't have the energy to work in my ministries anymore."

She paused, then asked the really important question: "But what will God think of me if I quit?"

Ashley was an exhausted frazzle. If you think I'm exaggerating in my description of her, I invite you to look around our churches today. Ask yourself how much sincere work is being done by joyless people who are doing it because of guilt, pressure, or manipulation, or in the effort to gain or retain God's acceptance.

"I'll tell you what God will think about you if you quit," I replied to Ashley. "He will love you with a perfect, eternal, never-changing love, the same love that took Jesus to the cross for you.

"And I'll tell you another thing," I continued, "God will *accept* you *just like you are*, even if you never do an ounce of service again. He loves you and wants a relationship with you, and he wants you to bask in his love every single day of your life. He doesn't love and accept you *because* you serve him. He only wants service that he initiates. God will never love or accept you one ounce more, or one ounce less, than he does right this minute. In Christ, you *are* accepted!"

We are not to be programmed by people, but led by the Spirit of God on a personal basis. God leads us individually—we are not cookie-cutter Christians.

My goal is not to stop Christians from serving. In fact, just the opposite! We follow a Lord who said of himself, "The Son of Man did *not* come to *be* served, but *to serve*, and to *give* his life as a ransom for many" (Matthew 20:28). Anyone who is genuinely following Jesus as his disciple (which means "learner" or "pupil") will be learning to adopt a servant's attitude as well. What I am dedicated to doing is helping believers learn to serve through the motivation of grace and the power of Christ living in them. Ashley was doing neither. Her drive to "serve" had actually become a desperate attempt to gain acceptance.

Ashley's story has been reproduced thousands of times over. A sincere believer begins following Christ and wants to serve him out of love and gratitude. Then, just as a ship accumulates barnacles, they start accumulating the beliefs, practices, and often, sheer nonsense of the Christians around them. Enjoyable time spent reading God's Word gradually turns into a required ritual. Joyful service becomes a duty, then a job, then drudgery. Eager desire to be among God's people becomes an obligation to go to church every time the doors are open. Eventually, their loving heavenly Father becomes a stern taskmaster scrutinizing them to determine whether they are "doing enough." I've lived it. Many of you reading this have lived it. It is a far cry from the "abundant life" Jesus Christ came to give us. A free, joyful relationship has been forgotten. Legalism reigns in its place.

What is the lure of legalism? People who do not understand the grace of God will inevitably think the Law is a ladder to climb up in their attempt to earn God's acceptance through performance, obedience, commitment, or self-discipline. It doesn't matter that the Lord never intended it to be used that way—it's just the way we fallen human beings are wired. If it isn't God's Law we're trying to live up to, it will be human laws we create and impose on ourselves and others. This tendency is incurable, except by New Covenant understanding.

Love *and* Acceptance

"But don't people know that God loves them?" some ask. Yes, many people do, but it's not as simple as that. I've had the experience many times of sharing Bible verses about God's love with people—John 3:16

for example. You may know how it starts: "God so loved the world that he gave his one and only Son—" I've had people interrupt me impatiently, "Yeah, yeah, I know that." One guy responded, "God loves everybody—big deal. He has to. He's God. It's his job."

How could the love of God become an idea of little relevance in some people's minds? It's because apart from the assurance of *acceptance*, love becomes purely theoretical in their hearts—just an intellectual concept that doesn't touch the emotions.

I remember when this insight first hit me. When my son, Bob, was a teenager, he and some buddies had gotten a supply of beer to celebrate the last day of school. I came home to find Amy crying and Bob sitting on the couch, looking green as the Grinch and sick as a dog. It was the first time he had tried drinking, and it had definitely made an impression. He had thrown up everything but his toenails.

I felt compassion more than anything else at the time. I put my arm around him and said, "Bobby, I love you. I don't like what you did, but I love you."

He looked at me with bleary eyes and said, "Dad, can we pray?" We did.

Bob later said to me, "Dad, I always knew you loved me. I've never seriously doubted it. But that day is when I really believed that you *accepted* me."

Our experience of God's love is the same. We can hear and read all the Bible verses in the world telling us about God's *love*, but they remain mostly theoretical until they are connected to his *acceptance*. God's love was concretely demonstrated in Jesus' death on the cross, where he acted to secure our complete acceptance in Christ.

This message is found only in the gospel of Jesus Christ and his New Covenant. The systems and values of the world around us constantly reinforce the assumption that acceptance must be earned or deserved. Consider the culture around you. Acceptance is offered on the basis of your achievements, abilities, or appearance. The common denominator of that kind of acceptance is that *those things can be taken away from you in the blink of an eye*. No wonder people live in fear!

In my years in ministry I have counseled thousands of individuals, not to mention the thousands more I've talked with on live radio. Based on my experience, I believe there are few things in the world more damaging for people than living and laboring under conditional acceptance—that is, where the message is "I accept you *if...*" "...*if* you are good enough...smart enough...beautiful enough ... perform enough...*if* you keep making me happy...*if* I'm still satisfied in our relationship." Families built on conditional acceptance mangle human hearts and warp human souls. Churches that teach and practice legalism can do the same.

As I've said, God gave Israel the Law to be their teacher and protector, not so they would actually try to earn his acceptance through law-keeping. He gave it to lead them to faith and a relationship with him. After the Old Covenant, the Lord announced the new and better covenant. In it we see God's unconditional, unilateral promise of *acceptance* and a *relationship* in Christ. This relationship rests upon *his* actions, not ours—upon *his* faithfulness, not ours! What better news could there be in the world? Humanity is looking for all these things to come from others, but only God can satisfy our deepest longings.

God Reveals His Secret

The word *unconditional* raises questions. Does that mean that *everyone* is in on it? If there are really no conditions, that would seem to follow. However, that can't be true, or everyone in the world would be saved. But if not everyone is in on it, then how *do* you come under this New Covenant with God?

There is another, related question we must handle first, one raised in the very promise of the New Covenant. The clause we are considering says, "I will be *their* God, and *they* will be my people." But *who* is meant by "their" and "they"? The Lord will be *whose* God? *Who* will be his people? In introducing his promise, he says,

> "The days are coming," declares the LORD, "when I will make a new covenant with the people of Israel and with the people of Judah" (Jeremiah 31:31).

The Lord says this New Covenant will be specifically with "Israel" and "Judah." What about the rest of the world? While there have been untold thousands of Jewish Christians since the first century, they are still a small minority compared to the Gentiles (non-Jews) who have believed in Christ. What about them?

Paul writes about this in his letter to the Ephesians. He says,

> Surely you have heard about the administration of God's grace that was given to me for you, that is, *the mystery made known to me by revelation*, as I have already written briefly. In reading this, then, you will be able to understand my insight into *the mystery of Christ* (Ephesians 3:2-4).

Here Paul states he has received direct revelation from God, and he describes the content of it as a "mystery." In our modern world, a mystery can refer to a puzzle, such as a "whodunit." Many television shows, for example, depict detectives working to solve murder mysteries. Or it can mean something "mysterious" or incomprehensible, a word we use for things we don't understand.

In the New Testament, however, the word *mystery* has a specific meaning. It refers to a secret hidden in the heart of God, but now revealed through God's chosen spokesmen. Paul explains this in the phrase immediately after he refers to "the mystery of Christ," saying that it

> was not made known to people in other generations as it has now been revealed by the Spirit to God's holy apostles and prophets (verse 5).

By a *mystery* the Bible means something previously secret that is now revealed. It actually means the opposite of our common usage. When most people today use the word, they mean something that is *not* understandable. But when the Bible speaks of a mystery, it means something that is made perfectly clear and revealed to all.

Most important, though, is the content of the mystery. What is it? Paul continues:

> This mystery is that through the gospel *the Gentiles are heirs together with Israel,* members together of one body, and sharers together in the promise in Christ Jesus (Ephesians 3:6).

Through the prophets of the Old Covenant, God promised a New Covenant with his people Israel. But God also had a secret all along. He had always intended to extend this New Covenant beyond Israel, making *all people who trust in Christ equal members of the body and equal heirs of the promises.*

This was not entirely new. The Old Testament contains dozens of passages where the Lord says the whole world will benefit and be blessed when the kingdom of God comes.

He had promised to Abraham hundreds of years before the Law, "*All peoples on earth* will be blessed through you" (Genesis 12:3). Isaiah told Israel of a future day when "nations will come to your light, and kings to the brightness of your dawn" (Isaiah 60:3). The prophet had also said,

> In that day the Root of Jesse [the Messiah] will stand as a banner for the peoples; *the nations will rally to him,* and his resting place will be glorious (Isaiah 11:10).

No, it was not a new idea that the entire world would be blessed when the Messiah brought his kingdom. But *nowhere in the Old Testament do you find the teaching that the Gentiles will be **equal heirs** with Israel in Christ in one body. That was God's secret, only revealed through the apostles after Jesus' death and resurrection.

The Guarantee of the Holy Spirit

If you believe in Christ, the Holy Spirit has raised you to life and come to indwell you forever. He is your comfort, your power, and the means by which Christ lives his life in and through you. What many believers have not seen, though, is that the presence of the Holy Spirit is God's promise to us of the security of our relationship.

Paul wrote,

> It is God who makes both us and you stand firm in Christ.
> He anointed us, set his seal of ownership on us, and put his
> Spirit in our hearts as a deposit, guaranteeing what is to
> come (2 Corinthians 1:21-22).

The word *deposit* can also be translated as "down payment" or "earnest." Both of those words are used commonly in the real-estate business to describe *a partial payment and a promise to complete the transaction.* That is what God is saying to us. He has bought us through the death of Christ, and we are secured in and through him. But we have not yet received everything we will receive in Christ. We are still waiting for new, immortal bodies like his to go with the new spiritual life we already have. The Holy Spirit, therefore, represents the promise of God that he will complete the process and transform our weak bodies into undying glorious ones in which we can live with him forever (1 Corinthians 15:42-53).

Paul argues along these lines when he scolds the Galatians, who were flirting with returning to the Law for the basis of their acceptance: "You foolish Galatians! Who has bewitched you?" (Galatians 3:1). Then he mentions the decisive proof that such a move is completely ridiculous:

> I would like to learn just one thing from you: Did you receive
> the Spirit by the works of the law, or by believing what you
> heard? Are you so foolish? After beginning by means of the
> Spirit, are you now trying to finish by means of the flesh?
> (Galatians 3:2-3).

That they possessed the Holy Spirit was the ultimate proof of God's acceptance. Why would they need anything else?

The same is true of you if you belong to Christ. His death for you was the completely sufficient sacrifice that cleansed you so that God could take up residence in you. You now have his life in you—you are his and he is yours. You are a now a temple of the Holy Spirit (1 Corinthians 6:19). You are a dwelling place of God himself. That could never have happened if you had not first been totally cleansed by the blood of Jesus Christ. So the Holy Spirit's presence is undeniable proof of God's complete and eternal acceptance of you in Christ!

Getting In on the New Covenant

It's time to consider the last questions on this subject I have posed but not answered. We have seen that God's promises in the New Covenant are unilateral and unconditional. How does one get in on this covenant? Are there any conditions at all?

Yes, there is one. Participation in the New Covenant is freely offered to you, but you are not forced into it. Your one decision is the choice to trust in Jesus Christ; that is, to believe, or have faith:

> God so loved the world that he gave his one and only Son,
> that *whoever believes in him* shall not perish but have eternal
> life (John 3:16).

Here is the best news ever proclaimed to the human race: Anyone who wishes can come to Jesus Christ on the basis of faith alone in him and enter into this New Covenant he has established by his death on the cross. That's it. You don't have to *do* anything to create, establish, or even maintain this covenant! All those things are the unilateral work and promise of God in Christ. All that is necessary for us is to believe the good news and trust in him. The completion and fulfillment of every promise is God's responsibility.

This is not to say we have no responsibilities *under* the covenant. We have many responsibilities as we walk with the Lord, learning from him and allowing Christ to live through us. *But it is not our responsibility to maintain or complete the provisions of the New Covenant. They are all the work of God, and we receive them all in Christ.*

God said, "I will be their God, and they will be my people." If you trust in Jesus Christ, then you can claim that promise with absolute assurance. You are loved by God, accepted by God, and will be securely held by God forever.

Not surprisingly, Jesus said it best:

My sheep listen to my voice; I know them, and they follow me. I give them eternal life, and they shall never perish; no one can snatch them out of my hand. My Father, who has given them to me, is greater than all; no one can snatch them out of my Father's hand. I and the Father are one (John 10:27-30).

Our security, our acceptance, and our destiny do not rest on our ability to serve, strive, or hang on to God. They all rest upon his faithfulness to hold us secure forever.

That is real love. That is real acceptance. That is real security.

9

An Intimate Relationship with the Father

The Barriers Are Down

No longer will they teach their neighbor, or say to one another,
"Know the Lord," because they will
all know me, from the least of them to the greatest.
HEBREWS 8:11

The Jewish people have followed their rabbinical traditions for many hundreds of years, even scattered as they are throughout the nations of the world. In so doing, they are attempting to follow the command of the Law:

> These commandments that I give you today are to be upon your hearts. Impress them on your children. Talk about them when you sit at home and when you walk along the road, when you lie down and when you get up. Tie them as symbols on your hands and bind them on your foreheads. Write them on the doorframes of your houses and on your gates (Deuteronomy 6:6-9).

According to the New Covenant, this will not be necessary. He himself will ensure that all his people know him personally and intimately. That is an incredible privilege and blessing!

Look at it from another angle, however—there is something even more important: the answer to the question, "Does he know *us*?"

To illustrate, let's consider someone as well-known in America and throughout the world as anybody could be—the president of the United States. You would have to admit that just about everybody knows who he is. His name and photo would be recognized the world over. And most Americans, regardless of their political persuasion, would consider it the high point of a lifetime to be introduced and shake his hand.

So imagine the president is coming to your town, and you and I stand side by side hoping to see him. The streets are lined several deep with people wanting to catch a glimpse of the motorcade. The crowd erupts as the line of limousines comes into view. Like hundreds of others I wave and shout as they go by. Afterward, I tell you excitedly, "That was the president! I know who he is!" How impressed would you be? Not very. Who doesn't know who he is?

But let's change our story a little. The motorcade comes into view, and everyone cheers and waves. But this time, the president's limo screeches to a halt right in front of us. The window rolls down, and the president leans out. "Bob!" he calls out. "How're you doing? Come on over here!" The Secret Service agents talking into their headsets pull up the rope, allowing me to get through. As I walk to the limousine, the president gets out, then greets me with a big hug. "Bob, it's been ages! Hey, we've got to get together!" He pulls a card out of his pocket and starts writing. "I've got to go now, but here's my super-secret direct line. Call me later, and we'll make plans to get together. See you! Be sure to call!" The president gets back into his vehicle, and the procession continues down the road.

As I walk back under the rope barrier, what do you think now? You're thinking, "*You know the president! And he wants to see you!*" You'd have to admit that *now* you're impressed!

I think this is the kind of situation Paul has in mind when he catches himself mid-verse in Galatians 4:

> Formerly, when you did not know God, you were slaves to
> those who by nature are not gods. But now that you know
> God—*or rather are known by God*—how is it that you are
> turning back to those weak and miserable forces? Do you
> wish to be enslaved by them all over again? (Galatians
> 4:8-9).

In a sense, virtually everyone "knows God," if you mean that they know something *about* him. But really knowing him—and more important, *being known by him*—is something else entirely. This deeper and personal knowledge is what God promises his children under the New Covenant. And this is the basis for genuine Christian living.

Motivation for New Covenant Living

The only thing that legalistic religion cares about is whether people are doing on the outside what they are supposed to be doing. "Believe the right things, do the right things, and avoid the wrong things," says religion. "Get in line. Conform. Walk and talk like the rest of us—or else!"

Jesus had this kind of religion in mind when he scorched the Pharisees:

> Isaiah was right when he prophesied about you hypocrites;
> as it is written: "These people honor me with their lips, but
> their hearts are far from me. They worship me in vain; their
> teachings are merely human rules." You have let go of the
> commands of God and are holding on to human traditions
> (Mark 7:6-8).

As we saw in the last chapter, God has always looked upon the heart, not outward behavior. He has always sought a relationship with human beings of faith. Genuine Christian living is an inside-out life, where outward actions are motivated and empowered by an inner experience, our relationship with God from the heart.

This is what drove the apostle Paul. Having been accused of being a crazy man by some of his opponents, Paul proceeds to explain the source of his motives and power:

> **Christ's love compels us,** because we are convinced that one died for all, and therefore all died. And he died for all, *that those who live should no longer live for themselves but for him* who died for them and was raised again (2 Corinthians 5:14-15).

Paul isn't talking about some kind of puppet relationship where he is forced against his will to live for God. When he says he is "compelled" he is saying he is irresistibly moved by his knowledge and experience of Christ's love so that he is *willingly driven* to live for him. "I can't help myself," Paul is saying. "Christ's love has become an irresistible force in my life." In his promise of the New Covenant, God also focuses on the inward:

> No longer will they teach their neighbor, or say to one another, "Know the LORD," because they will all know me, from the least of them to the greatest (Jeremiah 31:34).

If you have put your faith in Jesus Christ, then this is part of your inheritance as a child of God. This intimate, experiential knowledge of him as your Father has been made available to every person who enters into the New Covenant.

From Systematic Exclusions to Genuine Equality

The majority of the pagan religions of the world emphasize distinctions between people, with the idea that certain priests, mediums, shamans, or gurus are more in touch with the "spirits" or occult "powers" than ordinary folk. The Old Covenant itself reinforced the idea of some people being "closer to God" than others.

Recall, for example, that the Law of Moses dictated that one tribe, the Levites, were set aside as the priests of Israel. Members of other tribes need not apply. There were also places and items set aside as holy—most importantly, the physical structure and space of the Tabernacle and the later Temple. Other people, items, and places were therefore considered ordinary or everyday—even "unclean" under certain provisions of the Law.

But now the Lord says through Jeremiah that there will be a day when every one of his people is equal in status, privilege, and intimacy of relationship with him. As we turn to the teachings of the apostles in the New Testament, we find the wonderful truth that every barrier under the Old Covenant is specifically broken down in the New Covenant.

The first and most important truth is that anyone who believes in Christ becomes a child of God:

> To all who did receive him, to those who believed in his name, he gave the right to become children of God— children born not of natural descent, nor of human decision or a husband's will, but born of God (John 1:12-13).

What could be more wonderful than to know that you are a child of God? It is because of this that Jesus taught us to address God the Father as *Abba*—"Papa" or "Daddy"—the intimate term in Aramaic for "Father." The apostle Paul also emphasizes our status as God's children:

> You are all children of God through faith, for all of you who were baptized into Christ have clothed yourselves with Christ (Galatians 3:26-27).

Paul then goes on to show that this Father-child relationship supersedes all earthly, man-made measures of status and distinction:

> There is neither Jew nor Gentile, neither slave nor free, nor is there male and female, for you are all one in Christ Jesus (verse 28).

In his letter to the Colossians, Paul writes a parallel verse, adding a few more details:

> Here there is no Gentile or Jew, circumcised or uncircumcised, barbarian, Scythian, slave or free, but Christ is all, and is in all (Colossians 3:11).

This teaching was as shocking in the first century as it is today, if not more so. There is little in our everyday lives that prepares us for the radical nature of what the Lord has done through Christ in the New Covenant.

The Temple, remember, was a physical picture of progressive barriers between the world and God. Let's take a brief walk through the breaking down of those barriers under the New Covenant, and explore what the Lord is trying to teach us about ourselves.

No Distinction Between Jews and Gentiles

God was always interested in the whole world, and this is taught throughout the Old Testament, as we have previously seen. In the Temple the outer court was known as the "Court of the Gentiles" and—in theory, at least—anyone was free to come there to learn about God and worship. The Israelites, unfortunately, treated the Lord as a private possession and personal privilege, rather than seeing themselves as a "nation of priests" to the world. When Jesus famously overturned the tables in the Temple (Mark 11:15-17), it was because the money lenders—permitted by the religious leaders—had made a mockery of this area that was set aside for non-Jews. "Is it not written: 'My house will be called a house of prayer for *all nations*'?" he demanded of them, quoting Isaiah. "But you have made it 'a den of robbers,'" he concluded, this time quoting Jeremiah.

Now, however, in the New Covenant, Paul says "there is no Gentile or Jew, circumcised or uncircumcised" (Colossians 3:11). The word *Gentile* stood for any non-Jew at the time, especially those who were considered "civilized."

To the people of Israel, no distinction was more important. Their beliefs, lifestyle—even their own bodies—spoke loudly and continually that Israelites were "set apart," or "holy." All those outside were considered "dogs" because of their ignorance and filthy habits. But Christ has eliminated the barrier, which Paul spells out in another passage:

> Now in Christ Jesus you who once were far away [the Gentiles] have been brought near through the blood of Christ.

> For he himself is our peace, who has made the two
> groups one *and has destroyed the barrier, the dividing*
> *wall of hostility, by setting aside in his flesh the law with its*
> *commands and regulations.* His purpose was to create in
> himself one new humanity out of the two, thus making peace,
> and in one body to reconcile both of them to God through
> the cross, by which he put to death their hostility (Ephesians
> 2:13-16).

Notice that Paul explicitly refers to the physical wall in the Temple, indicating that it symbolized the separation of Jew from Gentile by the Law of Moses. Just think about it practically: Jews and Gentiles could never be united as long as the Old Covenant continued to be in effect, because it was the Law of Moses itself that formed the wall of separation between them. But God has destroyed the barrier by taking away the Law, so he could create one unified body of Christ.

In Colossians 3:11, Paul accentuates his point by also mentioning "barbarians" and "Scythians." In the Mediterranean world, barbarians were those peoples who did not speak Greek or adopt Greek culture, such as the Celtic and Germanic tribes of northern Europe. The Scythians were even worse, being fierce and uncivilized tribes who lived beyond the Black Sea. In the view of that time, Scythians represented the wildest types of barbarians, almost subhuman. But Paul says that in Christ there is no distinction. People of every kind are equal members of the New Covenant, and these external cultural differences do not matter.

First-century Jewish Christians found this new revelation very hard to swallow, and there are numerous passages in the New Testament that describe their difficulty coming to terms with it. That's why Paul spends so much time spelling out that "the Gentiles are heirs together with Israel, members together of one body, and sharers together in the promise in Christ Jesus" (Ephesians 3:6).

No Distinction Based on Social Status

Modern historians estimate that in the Roman Empire of the first century, at least 50 percent of the population were slaves. The dehumanizing and often brutal practice of slavery scars human history in every era and on every continent, and still persists today in parts of the world. Where slavery no longer is practiced as an institution, we still have the injustices and abuses of virtual slavery—economic, for instance. Human society as a matter of course builds social distinctions between the wealthy and poor, between the educated and uneducated, and between races and ethnic groups.

But now, in Christ, there is no distinction. The revolutionary nature of the gospel can be seen here in how it subverted and eventually transformed Roman society. The New Testament writings show masters and slaves worshipping side by side in house churches. Early historical accounts tell of individual slaves gaining influence in the church to the point where they served in leadership over aristocrats.

Besides the blurring of the classes, the teaching of the apostles changed the way people thought about social and economic status. In answering some questions from the church at Corinth, Paul teaches them that these external social markings are not that important:

> Were you a slave when you were called? Don't let it trouble you—although if you can gain your freedom, do so. For the one who was a slave when called to faith in the Lord is the Lord's freed person; similarly, the one who was free when called is Christ's slave (1 Corinthians 7:21-22).

"It's all right to gain your freedom if you can," says Paul to slaves. "But don't worry about it. You are free in Christ." Then he puts free men and women in their place: "You also are 'slaves' of Christ." Speaking in another passage to both slaves and masters, Paul says,

> Slaves, obey your earthly masters with respect and fear, and with sincerity of heart, just as you would obey Christ...And masters, treat your slaves in the same way. Do not threaten them, since you know that he who is both their Master and yours is in heaven, and there is no favoritism with him (Ephesians 6:5,9).

Neither Christ nor the apostles led a frontal assault on the evils of slavery or social injustice. But by teaching that all people are equal as children of God through Jesus Christ, they brought about an invisible revolution in people's thinking that led to visible results. They still do. Where the gospel genuinely hits home in people's hearts, they realize that racism, bigotry, class pride, snobbery, and social injustice are completely contrary to the will and heart of God.

No Distinction Between Male and Female

After Jewish people passed through the wall barring Gentiles from entry, they came into what was known as the "Court of the Women." The reason, naturally, is that Jewish women along with men could participate there. But once again, this privilege had a limit. Women would come to another wall, which barred the way to them forward from that point. Only Jewish men could continue into the Court of Israel.

The next shocking thing Paul says is that in Christ "there is neither male nor female" (Galatians 3:28 ESV). There is no advantage whatsoever in being a man over being a woman. In the New Covenant we have exactly the same privileges and status.

In another prophecy of the New Covenant, quoted by Peter in his first public sermon on Pentecost (Acts 2:16-21), we find this same emphasis:

> I will pour out my Spirit on all people. Your sons and daughters will prophesy, your young men will see visions, your old men will dream dreams. Even on my servants, both men and women, I will pour out my Spirit in those days (Joel 2:28-29).

Once again, we know that in this world, equality of privilege, status, and rights are hard to come by. This is certainly true of the relationship between the sexes. But in the New Covenant, women, as well as men, can claim their full rights as children of God and come to him to enjoy an intimate Father–child relationship. The gift of the Holy Spirit has been given to all believers in Christ equally.

No Distinction Between Priests and Laymen

The final wall in the Temple separated ordinary Israelite men from the "Court of the Priests." Unless you were a Levite of the right lineage, you had to stop there. Only qualified priests could offer sacrifices on the altar or wash in the laver of cleansing. Others could only watch from afar.

At this point, distinctions among the priests themselves also became evident. Only certain priests were qualified to serve inside the sanctuary proper, the Holy Place. And beyond this point, everyone stopped save the High Priest alone. On only one day each year, the Day of Atonement, the High Priest could enter beyond the veil separating the outer room from the Holy of Holies. In this most sacred room was the Ark of the Covenant, which represented the throne of God, and above which he manifested his presence. Apart from the following exact procedures God had outlined—most importantly, bringing the correct sacrificial blood—entering the Holy of Holies was an automatic death sentence.

But now, in the New Covenant, there is no distinction between persons, not even between priests and ordinary people!

> You also, like living stones are being built into a spiritual house *to be a holy priesthood*, offering spiritual sacrifices acceptable to God through Jesus Christ…You are a chosen people, *a royal priesthood*, a holy nation, God's special possession, that you may declare the praises of him who called you out of darkness into his wonderful light (1 Peter 2:5,9).

The apostle John begins the book of Revelation similarly, with a benediction to God and the Lord Jesus Christ:

> To him who loves us and has freed us from our sins by his blood, and *has made us to be a kingdom and priests* to serve his God and Father—to him be glory and power for ever and ever! Amen (Revelation 1:5-6).

In John's later description of the heavenly celebration in honor of Christ, those who are present sing,

> You are worthy to take the scroll and to open its seals, because you were slain, and with your blood you purchased

for God persons from every tribe and language and people
and nation. *You have made them to be a kingdom and
priests to serve our God,* and they will reign on the earth
(Revelation 5:9-10).

As a result of Christ's finished work on the cross, we have been made
a whole kingdom of priests. That means we need no human represen-
tative to serve between us and God. And Christ himself is our high
priest—we need no other. He is the one who has died to purchase our
redemption and provide forgiveness of sins. He is the one who gave us
his life—eternal life. He is the fulfillment of the Day of Atonement:
"He has appeared once for all at the culmination of the ages to do away
with sin by the sacrifice of himself" (Hebrews 9:26).

Now of course, while we are in this life, we are often weak and need
the encouragement of others. In fact, we are often told to look out for
one another, encourage one another, and "carry each other's burdens"
(Galatians 6:2). This is part of the work you and I are privileged to do as
members of Christ's body. But no one has an "in" or a "hotline" to get
God's attention and care that is not available to you. All this is the basis
of the doctrine known as "the priesthood of the believer." Christians
have struggled to understand and practice this truth over the last 20
centuries. We have continued to elevate leaders to the status of "clergy,"
while the rest of us are just the "laity," but none of this comes from the
Scriptures. Every believer is a priest with full privileges in Christ Jesus.

Free Access for All Believers

Jesus accomplished it all! When he died on the cross, "At that
moment the curtain in the temple was torn in two from top to bot-
tom" (Matthew 27:51). This supernatural event was God's emphatic
statement that the Old Covenant was over, that sin had been dealt
with and that, amazingly, *the way into God's very presence is open to all
through faith in Jesus Christ.* The writer of Hebrews teaches us that the
veil itself represented the body of Jesus—that its tearing represented
his death for us:

> Since *we have confidence to enter the Most Holy Place by the blood of Jesus,* by a new and living way opened for us through the curtain, that is, his body, and since we have a great priest over the house of God, *let us draw near to God* with a sincere heart and with the full assurance that faith brings, having our hearts sprinkled to cleanse us from a guilty conscience and having our bodies washed with pure water (Hebrews 10:19-22).

Every believer is now urged to walk in the truth of this great privilege that Christ has purchased for us. Imagine—people were once told they would die for unlawfully entering the Most Holy Place, but now the most humble, ordinary Christian is encouraged to draw near to God, to get to know him as Father, and to receive his grace and power:

> Let us then approach God's throne of grace with confidence, so that we may receive mercy and find grace to help us in our time of need (Hebrews 4:16).

This invitation is for everyone. Not even the apostle Paul claimed that he had greater access to God than any other believer. Every child of God in Christ—you, me, everyone—is a saint, a "holy one" in his sight. And every single one of us has this authority to approach him with boldness and confidence.

Open Your Heart to the Love of Christ

The Bible is clear that all Christians have equal authority to enter the presence of God boldly, but we also know that not all of us do so. Why? In some cases, it is lack of knowledge. People who simply don't know about the blessings of the New Covenant cannot take full advantage of them. There are, however, many people who have heard good teaching or have read the New Testament for themselves—people who have heard about these truths, but still would say these promises are not real in their experience. They tend to rely on their own understanding instead of acknowledging God in all their ways. If we do this, God promised that he would make our paths straight.

What about you? If you are in that boat, I hope by now you have learned a great deal about the inheritance Christ has purchased for you, and that you have a growing hunger to experience for yourself all that God wants to give you. What now? We need to get to know God and his character and personality more and more.

Most of us have learned that it's not enough to have knowledge in our heads. Many Christians already have more solid Bible teaching and resources at their disposal than any Christian generation in history. But I don't see any evidence that we are any more successful in living it out than previous generations—it looks more like the opposite. We need *heart knowledge* in order to have a change of life.

Paul knew this, certainly, and that is why he pauses so often in his letters and prays for believers. For example, in his theologically jam-packed letter to the Ephesians, Paul pauses twice in the first three chapters to pray for those who would hear his teaching. To be specific, Paul prays for more than intellectual understanding. He prays that

> the *eyes of your heart may be enlightened* in order that you may know the hope to which he has called you, the riches of his glorious inheritance in his holy people, and his incomparably great power for us who believe (Ephesians 1:18-19).

Again, in the third chapter, Paul relates his prayer for the Ephesians. I have always found this prayer to be the best expression of the disposition of the person who genuinely comes to "hear the music"—that is, gains the life-transforming spiritual understanding of the love of Jesus Christ. Let's walk through it together a step at a time.

Paul has spent two chapters teaching about Christ's accomplishment and our resulting inheritance in him. Now he says,

> For this reason I kneel before the Father, from whom every family in heaven and on earth derives its name. I pray that

out of his glorious riches he may strengthen you with power
through his Spirit in your inner being... (Ephesians 3:14-16).

Because of God's "glorious riches," he has superabundant power
and grace to share with us. It's a reminder that we need not fear he'll
run low on his supplies. The Lord's ability to cause us to overflow with
blessings can never be exhausted. From that infinite source, Paul prays
that the Father will "strengthen" us "through his Spirit." Every believer
has been indwelt by the Holy Spirit, who regenerated us at the moment
we believed. With new spiritual life and Christ living in us, we have
access to this power in our "inner being."

Letting Christ Be at Home in Your Heart

Everybody's interested in power. Many want to do miracles. Many
want to overcome problems in life. But when Paul prays for power, it's
power for what? Few of us would quickly think of what he has in mind:

...so that Christ may dwell in your hearts through faith (verse
17).

It is common among Christians to talk about "asking Jesus to come
into your heart," especially with children. Almost always, that language is a reference to a person's acceptance of Christ as Savior—that
is, becoming saved. Be sure you notice, however, that this is not what
Paul means here. He is writing to churches where he assumes virtually
everyone has already trusted in Christ as Savior. He assumes he is talking to Christians. Therefore, he means something else.

Doesn't Christ already dwell in the hearts of believers? Yes, if you
are referring to the indwelling of the Holy Spirit. But that's not what
Paul is talking about. He is talking about the *status*, you might say, or
intimacy that Christ has in the hearts of his people.

What Paul is praying in this passage is that we will grant Jesus Christ
the status of a familiar guest in our hearts. He is welcome to come in
as Lord of the premises, but a Lord with whom we have the most intimate family relationship. He can say what he wants, do what he wants,
go where he wants. He can wander the halls and open closed doors.

There are none locked to him, no places where we want him to mind his own business. The entirety of our hearts is his home and his business. This is when we fulfill the famous offer Jesus made to the believers in the church at Laodicea:

> Here I am! I stand at the door and knock. If anyone hears my voice and opens the door, I will come in and eat with that person, and they with me (Revelation 3:20).

Though this verse has been used uncounted times as an invitation to people to receive Christ as their Savior (and that is fine), its real meaning in context is an invitation to people who are already Christians—to open their hearts to an intimate relationship with Christ.

You'll notice that Paul prays that we'll be "strengthened" to grant Christ this status. That's because of the ongoing struggle we all still face with the sin in our flesh. The natural tendency of the flesh is to resist him and want to do our own thing, but by the power of the Spirit we can grow in this direction.

Filled with All God's Fullness

Finally, Paul explains the end result he hopes for us. When we open our hearts to Christ personally, something even more wonderful can follow:

> And I pray that you, being rooted and established in love, may have power, together with all the Lord's holy people, to grasp how wide and long and high and deep is the love of Christ, and to know this love that surpasses knowledge—that you may be filled to the measure of all the fullness of God (Ephesians 3:17-19).

Here is the knowledge that changes lives. To be convinced of and to know the love of Christ that surpasses knowledge we need the power of the Holy Spirit. And the Lord is not reluctant. I am convinced that he wants every child of God to know this transforming experience. The result of being filled up to the fullness of God is unpredictable, except that it will be predictably wonderful. Paul says afterward that God "is able to do immeasurably more than all we ask or imagine, according to his power that is at work within us" (verse 20).

The Lord's ability to transform your life is beyond your ability to conceive. Open the New Testament and ask him to help you understand what Christ has done and who you are—your identity—as a result. Pray this prayer for yourself. Invite Christ to be fully at home in your heart. Ask the Lord to open your mind and heart to understand how great is his love for you. He will be eager to answer your prayer, and it may be the beginning for you of a whole new kind of life and love.

10

Total Forgiveness

Done Perfectly, Completely, Once-for-All

I will forgive their wickedness and will remember their sins no more.
JEREMIAH 31:34

In my more than 35 years of ministry, the most pressing and important question on people's minds has to do with God's forgiveness. This is because, by and large, believers have not settled the issue of what Christ has accomplished on the cross.

With a little thought you can see that it must be so. If I cannot be sure my sins are totally and forever forgiven, how can I be secure in the knowledge that God loves and accepts me? If I cannot be secure in God's love and acceptance, how can I rest in my relationship with him?

If I cannot rest in Christ's finished work on the cross, then I will have to continue working in some way to try to gain assurance. The New Covenant promise of the complete and final forgiveness of sins therefore is the foundation. It is the promise that guarantees the others.

The Promise that Guarantees the Others

In every age the tendency of believers is to drift from their understanding of Jesus Christ, his finished work on the cross, and the life that is lived by faith in his New Covenant. The letter to the Hebrews still speaks clearly to those of us who struggle to comprehend and rest in the immensity of Christ's accomplishment. No other book of the Bible so powerfully and comprehensively presents the completeness and meaning of Jesus' death on the cross.

That's why I want to rely heavily on Hebrews as we explore the final promise in the New Covenant. The Lord said,

> Their sins and lawless acts I will remember no more (Hebrews 10:17).

It is interesting that in both Jeremiah 31 and in Hebrews, which is quoting the Old Testament prophet, the Lord saved this promise for last. In one sense it is the one that makes the other three promises of the New Covenant (which we've covered in the previous three chapters) possible. Apart from final and complete forgiveness of sins, we could not be regenerated to eternal life, be unconditionally accepted, or enjoy a secure, intimate relationship with our heavenly Father. Apart from final and complete forgiveness of sins, all of those things would remain merely potential and temporary, at best.

If any of our sins were unforgiven in God's sight, we would remain under the rule of "the wages of sin," which is *death*. For us to receive *life* that can be described as "eternal," complete forgiveness of sins is a necessity. Because of the New Covenant promise of unconditional forgiveness, the apostle Paul could write,

> The wages of sin is death, but *the gift of God is eternal life in Christ Jesus our Lord* (Romans 6:23).

If we as Christians are not totally forgiven, then we cannot trust that we have eternal life or that our relationship and acceptance with our Father are secure. As a result, we cannot rest in our mind and in our daily life. This is an absolutely critical issue to understand and settle in our own minds if we want to be free to live as God wants us to in this world.

These truths are also right at the core of understanding the importance of distinguishing the Old Covenant, the Law of Moses, from
the New Covenant. After all we have explored together in the previous
chapters, look again at a key passage we touched on before. Previously
I emphasized the descriptions of the Old Covenant. This time, pay
particular attention to the descriptions of the New. Paul says that God

> has made us competent as ministers of a *new covenant*—
> not of the letter but of the *Spirit;* for the letter kills, but *the
> Spirit gives life.*
>
> Now if the ministry that brought death, which was engraved
> in letters on stone, came with glory…will not *the ministry of
> the Spirit* be even more glorious? If the ministry that brought
> condemnation was glorious, how much more glorious is *the
> ministry that brings righteousness!* (2 Corinthians 3:6-7,8-9).

Paul clearly positions himself as a "New Covenant man" in this
passage, knowing that this distinction is central to understanding
the gospel itself. The New Covenant is called "the ministry of the
Spirit" that "gives life"—Christ's life, which is eternal—and "brings
righteousness"—a righteousness that comes by faith and is from God.
All this in direct contrast to the Old Covenant which "kills," "brought
death," and "brought condemnation." (How can anyone say that this
is not a critical issue for biblical understanding?)

There are dozens of passages in both testaments—and we've looked
at many of them—that outline the differences between the covenants
and the superiority and finality of the New Covenant. But the book
of Hebrews shines the brightest light on this difference and brings the
superiority of the New Covenant into clearest view.

The Supremacy of Jesus Christ

The writer of Hebrews starts his contrast of the Old and New in the
very first verse of his letter:

> In the past God spoke to our ancestors through the prophets
> at many times and in various ways, *but* in these last days he
> has spoken to us by his *Son*... (Hebrews 1:1-2).

God's past messages through the prophets, in what we call the Old Testament, were a progressive unfolding of the Lord's words to humanity over many centuries and through dozens of different writers. But now God has "given his final word" through Jesus Christ, his Son. From the start, the author emphasizes the superiority and finality of God's work in Christ. The Father's revelation through Jesus Christ is not just one more in a long, progressive delivery of the Word of God. He is the Word of God made flesh, as John says in his Gospel (John 1:1-3,14). Hebrews continues:

> ...whom he appointed heir of all things; and through whom
> also he made the universe. The Son is the radiance of God's
> glory and the exact representation of his being, sustaining
> all things by his powerful word (verses 2-3).

No, Jesus is not just another in God's long line of prophets. He is God the Son himself. The writer uses truly mind-blowing descriptions to emphasize Jesus' deity. While the first verse of the Bible says, "In the beginning God created the heavens and the earth" (Genesis 1:1), here we are told that the Son was God's agent in creating all things. Not only that, but he is the "exact representation" of God's being and nature. Having created all things, the Son continues to hold all things together.

The writer could hardly have used more powerful descriptions to assert that Jesus is God himself, the Second Person of the Trinity. He goes on then to speak of Jesus' work of redemption:

> After he had provided purification for sins, he sat down at
> the right hand of the Majesty in heaven. So he became as
> much superior to the angels as the name he has inherited is
> superior to theirs (Hebrews 1:3-4).

Having stated that Jesus Christ is superior to all others in his Person, the writer now asserts that Jesus' work of redemption in providing "purification for sins" is absolutely complete, proven by the fact that he "sat down" at the right hand of God. This work qualified the incarnate Christ to be declared Lord of all creation, infinitely superior to even the powerful angelic beings that serve God. If that is true, how much more is he superior to all earthly beings!

The implications of these verses expand and grow into the whole book of Hebrews. The writer stated his theme: Jesus Christ is better in every way to anything and anyone previously available under the Old Covenant, and this includes his sacrifice for sin. Through his death, the pouring out of his perfect and pure blood, Jesus did for us that which was impossible for the blood of bulls and goats to do. Christ is God's final and complete revelation to the human race, and his New Covenant has been inaugurated. The Old is obsolete and not an option.

What About the Old Covenant?

In light of this stunning revelation concerning the superiority of the New Covenant, you may be wondering about the relevance of the Old Testament. Does the Old Testament have anything for us as New Covenant believers?

Let me say it very plainly: Everything in the Old Testament points forward to Jesus Christ and to the New Covenant. Listen to what Jesus had to say concerning the Old Testament. After being raised from the dead, he met up with two of his disciples on the road to Emmaus. They were confused about the events that had transpired just the week before. Jesus' death was devastating to them. Jesus joined them in their journey and listened to their conversation. Then he said to them,

> O foolish ones, and slow of heart to believe all that the prophets have spoken! Was it not necessary that the Christ should suffer these things and enter into his glory? (Luke 24:25-26 ESV).

He then walked them through the Old Testament, explaining how the Scriptures spoke of him:

> And beginning with Moses and all the Prophets, he interpreted to them in all the Scriptures the things concerning Himself (verse 27 ESV).

In one of his many conversations with the Pharisees, Jesus said this to them:

> You study the Scriptures diligently because you think that in them you have eternal life. These are the very Scriptures that testify about me, yet you refuse to come to me to have life (John 5:39-40).

These religious leaders diligently studied the Old Testament. They knew what it said, but they did not know what it meant. If they had truly understood the Scriptures they would have embraced Jesus as their Messiah and would have turned to him for life.

When you and I fully embrace Jesus and live out his New Covenant promises, we uphold all that was written before and prove out its highest and most noble purpose. We have seen many examples so far, but here is one that relates to the book of Hebrews. The fact that Jesus sat down after his work in providing purification of sins was done is a fulfillment of Psalm 110:1:

> The LORD says to my Lord, "Sit at my right hand until I make your enemies a footstool for your feet."

David did not know exactly how this prophecy would be fulfilled. All he knew was that he was speaking of a future event. Peter noted this in his first letter. Concerning the writers of old he had this to say:

> Concerning this salvation, the prophets, who spoke of the grace that was to come to you, searched intently and with the greatest care, trying to find out the time and circumstances

to which the Spirit of Christ in them was pointing when he
predicted the sufferings of the Messiah and the glories that
would follow. It was revealed to them that they were not
serving themselves but you, when they spoke of the things
that have now been told you by those who have preached
the gospel to you by the Holy Spirit sent from heaven. Even
angels long to look into these things (1 Peter 1:10-12).

God revealed to David, Moses, Jeremiah, and all the Old Testament
writers that they were not serving themselves, but us. They knew the
grace they were speaking of was for a future generation—a time when
their words would become reality.

If any of these prophets could see and speak to us today, here is
what I believe they would do. First, after recovering from their shock
at the Gentiles and Jews being together in one body, they would turn
a few handsprings to see the fulfillment of the promises. David in particular would probably whoop and holler and dance. Then all of them
would encourage and even admonish us if necessary to embrace the
New Covenant and walk fully in the grace that is ours in Christ Jesus.
They would let us know they are honored that their words concerning
Jesus have found their fulfillment in us! We honor all that's gone before
us when we let go of the old and take hold of the new.

Jesus Christ's death put an end to the Old Covenant. He fulfilled
the Law in its entirety just as he said he would: "Do not think that I
have come to abolish the Law or the Prophets; I have not come to abolish them but to fulfill them" (Matthew 5:17). And his death cleared the
way for the New Covenant of grace.

The Inadequacy of Old-Covenant Forgiveness

Chapter 10 is the summit of the letter to the Hebrews, culminating
the teaching on the finished work of Jesus Christ and all that he accomplished for us on the cross. To make his point concerning the superiority of Christ's sacrifice, the writer compares it to the weakness of the
forgiveness available under the Old Covenant:

> The law is only a shadow of the good things that are coming—not the realities themselves. For this reason it can never, by the same sacrifices repeated endlessly year after year, make perfect those who draw near to worship. If it could, would they not have stopped being offered? For the worshipers would have been cleansed once for all, and would no longer have felt guilty for their sins (Hebrews 10:1-2).

We can see several key points. First, the Law was never the full reality of salvation; it was only a "shadow," or representation, of what God was going to do. For example, his Spirit came upon the saints of old to empower them to carry out specific duties and responsibilities, but he did not permanently indwell them as he does us. The Old Covenant taught people extremely important elementary truths and provided many pictures of the Lord and his saving work. But notice: It was "not the realities themselves."

Second, Old Covenant worshippers were never made "perfect." The proof is obvious—if they had been, then there would have been an end to the sacrifices. But this never happened; sacrifices under the Law of Moses were unending. There were daily sacrifices, weekly sacrifices, monthly sacrifices, and annual sacrifices, not to mention the special sacrifices demanded by the Law for various transgressions and mistakes. That's why the work of priests under the Law was never-ending.

Finally, forgiveness under the Old Covenant was never complete. At best, it offered a cleansing that brought a person up to date—in essence, made him again "an Israelite in good standing" under the Law. But as I pointed out in chapter 5, nowhere in the Law is there a promise of forgiveness for *tomorrow's* sins. That's why they were offered continually. Then the writer offers an interesting psychological insight:

> Those sacrifices are an annual reminder of sins (Hebrews 10:3).

No Relief of Conscience

Upon first considering the matter, you would probably guess that offering sacrifices according to the Law would bring relief. No doubt it did. But this verse tells us something more. Speaking of the most important sacrifices under the Law, those offered on the annual Day of Atonement, the writer says they were a "reminder of *sins*." Wouldn't you think they would be a reminder of forgiveness? The answer is yes and no.

In my second book, *Growing in Grace*, I related the true story of a young man I called Stewart who was driving drunk one night and killed an 18-year-old girl. The girl's family sued him in civil court and received a judgment of $1.5 million. They settled, however, for $936. If you were the guilty driver, wouldn't you think that was very good news? You probably would, but there was a catch: The money had to be paid at the rate of $1 per week for 18 years, representing the life of the girl who was killed. According to the judgment, every Friday, Stewart had to write out a $1 check in the name of the girl and mail it. As the news account reported, Stewart paid for a while, then stopped. The family went back to court, and he was ordered to resume payments. After a while he stopped again. Same result.

Finally, after several years, Stewart countersued. He called the $1-a-week payments "cruel and unusual punishment." He said he was "tormented" by the judgment. "I just want to get on with my life," he said, and he offered the family a whole box of prewritten $1 checks. "No," they replied firmly. "We want to receive those checks every week, or we'll go back to court."

There are extremely few people in the United States who would notice the loss of a single dollar every week. How do you account for Stewart's strong reaction and expressions of pain? Imagine yourself in his position. Each week you mail that check and feel some relief. *That's over for this week*, you think. But then on Monday you know in the back of your mind, *Friday's coming*. Tuesday, same thing. You start tightening up on Wednesday. Thursday your heart beats and your palms become moist as you anticipate another "black Friday." Every single week, round and round you go. Never able to forget. Never able to freely move on. Every week, the name of that girl is in the front of your mind, along with the hard faces of her family. There can be no once-and-for-all payment. Just mail in your $1 check, over and over again.

I think the writer of Hebrews has this kind of mental process in mind when he says that "those sacrifices are an annual reminder of *sins*." Yes, there is temporary relief, but tomorrow starts a new year. *My sins start adding up again*, people would think. There can never be an end under that system, as he explains, because

> it is impossible for the blood of bulls and goats to take away sins (Hebrews 10:4).

The Temporary Covering of Sins

"But if it is 'impossible,'" you might ask, "then how could there be forgiveness at all under the Law?"

What God did in anticipation of the death of Jesus Christ was to offer forgiveness on the basis of *atonement*. That word means "to cover." The author of Hebrews strongly asserts that animal sacrifices could not "*take away* sins," but they could and did "cover" them. Let's consider a credit card as an analogy. A credit card is worthless in and of itself. It's just a piece of plastic. But by convention and contract, it stands for a promise to pay. Let's say you see a nice new jacket at a store. You don't have enough money in your bank account, but you do have this handy little credit card in your pocket. (And realize, I don't recommend this habit.) You hand it over, sign your name, and walk out of the store with a new jacket—but you haven't paid a penny for it. That's the good news. The bad news is that there's a charge account with your name on it, growing somewhere. Sooner or later, somebody will have to pay that account.

That's the way "atonement" worked. The worshipper who believed God's Word and followed the procedure he had specified walked away with forgiveness up to the present, *but it had not been paid for*. The worshipper's sins had only been transferred to an "account." For centuries in the Old Testament period, God treated believing people as if they were forgiven, even though the "account" of people's sins was building up unpaid. Someone, someday, would have to pay it. Sins would have to be taken away.

Christ's Finished Work on the Cross

What the Law was unable to do, Jesus Christ accomplished. Hebrews 10 goes on:

> Therefore, when Christ came into the world, he said: "Sacrifice and offering you did not desire, but a body you prepared for me; with burnt offerings and sin offerings you were not pleased. Then I said, 'Here I am—it is written about me in the scroll—I have come to do your will, my God'" (Hebrews 10:5-7).

The internal quotation in these verses is from Psalm 40. We looked at this passage before as an example of David's acknowledging God's desire for worship that comes from the heart. However, we all know that every human being has fallen short of this ideal, no matter how much he or she loves God. But the Son of David, Jesus Christ, is the perfect fulfillment of these words. He alone of all the human race has loved God perfectly and done his will without fail.

In the case of Jesus, God's "will" was a specific mission. It meant taking upon himself the sins of the world and dying in our place. That is why his humanity shrank back from the horror of the cross. He prayed, "*Abba*, Father, everything is possible for you. Take this cup from me." We will give thanks for eternity that his prayer did not end there. He went on to say, "Yet not what I will, but what you will" (Mark 14:36). This is where the writer of Hebrews continues on to the high point of his teaching:

> And by that will, we have been made holy through the sacrifice of the body of Jesus Christ once for all (Hebrews 10:10).

In complete contrast to those Old Covenant sacrifices, which were offered "endlessly year after year" (verse 2), Jesus died "once for all"! And the result of his one sacrifice of himself is that we who are in Christ "have been made holy"!

To hammer home his point, the writer then contrasts the ongoing work of the Old Covenant priests versus that of Christ as the final high priest:

Day after day every priest stands and performs his religious duties; again and again he offers the same sacrifices, which can never take away sins. But when this priest had offered *for all time one sacrifice for sins, he sat down at the right hand of God*, and since that time he waits for his enemies to be made his footstool. For *by one sacrifice he has made perfect forever* those who are being made holy (verses 11-14).

This is truly one of the highest peaks in the mountain range of the New Testament. The Old Covenant priests are shown *standing*. Why? Because their work was never done! But Christ completed his work of offering "for all time one sacrifice for sins," and has therefore "sat down"—a clear reference to Psalm 110. He will never die again. He will never have to, because his death is infinitely sufficient. Those who trust in him are therefore "made perfect forever."

I wish every Christian would come to know, underline, memorize, and celebrate the truths contained in this passage of Scripture. Let them sink down into the depths of your soul. Because of Jesus' sacrifice, you have been made holy. You have been made perfect. All that you have been so desperate to achieve, yet have failed to do time and time again, is now yours in Christ. We walk by faith in this truth.

The New Covenant Promise Fulfilled

Therefore, the Lord's promise centuries before through Jeremiah has been fulfilled. The writer of Hebrews goes on to make this very point:

The Holy Spirit also testifies to us about this. First he says, "This is the covenant I will make with them after that time, says the Lord. I will put my laws in their hearts, and I will write them on their minds." Then he adds, "Their sins and lawless acts I will remember no more" (Hebrews 10:15-17).

The writer then puts an exclamation point on the truths he has expounded:

> And where these have been forgiven, sacrifice for sin is no longer necessary (verse 18).

The Jewish Christians who were the original recipients of this letter could not have missed the message. That Old Covenant was finished, obsolete, powerless. The choice for the Hebrew Christians of that day was confidence in Jesus Christ—or *nothing*.

The same is true for you and me. God has spoken and acted in his Son, Jesus Christ. There is no "Plan B" for those who will not receive what God has provided in him. But once we have seen all that has been offered to us in Christ, why would anyone want an alternative? In Jesus Christ we receive complete, once-and-for-all, eternal forgiveness of sins. We are made holy in God's sight. We are given the righteousness of Christ himself, a standing of perfect acceptability before a holy God who has become our Father. Throughout eternity we will discover all that he is and all that he has given us.

Let me be as clear as possible concerning forgiveness. Stand firm. You are a forgiven person. All your sins, past, present, and future, have been taken away. The apostle Paul put it this way:

> When you were dead in your sins and in the uncircumcision of your flesh, *God made you alive with Christ. He forgave us all our sins*, having canceled the charge of our legal indebtedness, which stood against us and condemned us; he has taken it away, nailing it to the cross (Colossians 2:13-14).

What does this mean? The sin you will commit tomorrow is already forgiven. You will feel sorry for that sin and the hurt it caused. You may even ask God to forgive it. His Spirit will answer emphatically: *God remembers your sins no more*. Let that truth sink in. Jesus declared in victory, "It is finished!" His death completed the Old Covenant. Forgiveness is yours.

Danny's Story

My friend Danny recently wrote to our ministry to share his story. Like so many others, he struggled with the forgiveness issue. Guilt haunted him and toyed with and tormented his mind to the point that he wondered whether he was even saved.

He had responded to the gospel, trusting Christ as his Lord and Savior, in 1984. Someone taught him at that time that every time he sinned, he needed to ask God to forgive that sin. It didn't make sense to him in light of the gospel message. As he wrote, "To say the least, I walked in confusion for three years about the sin issue. Fear and guilt were my lot, even fearing I might lose my salvation."

He read a booklet on self-esteem, and several points from it struck a chord in his heart. One in particular was this statement by the booklet's author: "Light began to break over me when I realized in the depths of my spirit that I was forgiven, cleansed, accepted, justified because of what Christ had done for me and not because of the depth of my yieldedness." This stayed with Danny, even though he didn't know fully what the statement meant. "It is finished" had yet to break through.

Three years later, Danny came across our radio broadcast. As I have mentioned, in the many years of our live call-in program, forgiveness has been the most discussed issue, and it was on-air conversations about the completeness of forgiveness that kept Danny tuned in. "I kept listening, and listening, and listening," he wrote. "Then one day at work, light began to break over me and I began to fully realize the meaning and fullness of 'It is finished!' At that moment, God revealed to me the completeness and totality of his forgiveness toward me.

"All I could do for the rest of my days was to thank the Lord Jesus over, and over, and over. I could feel the guilt leave me as though it had sprouted wings and flew away. And for the next seven days I felt such a wonderful and deep peace. I've never been the same since."

Danny had done everything in his power to gain forgiveness of sins. He had been faithful to carry out what he had been taught to do every time he sinned, yet just like those sacrifices in the Old Covenant, it did nothing to remove his guilt and fear. The sacrifices could not take away the sins of the people. Only Jesus has the authority and power to take away our sins, to forgive us. And he did, through his shed blood on the cross. When Danny rested in Christ's work, his life changed permanently. Today, as he writes, "I walk in peaceful freedom."

Christ's Accomplishment and Awesome Love

With forgiveness comes the realization that God truly loves you. The apostle John wrote that the one who fears is not made perfect in love. In context, the fear is fear of punishment (1 John 4:18). If you haven't settled the fact that Christ took the punishment for your sins, you will live each day in the fearful expectation of God's punishment. Living with this fear makes it impossible to truly know that he loves you.

This doubt and struggle will continue until you do rest in the finality of the cross. The moment you do, the love of God breaks through and you know it is real. This powerful love overtakes our human hearts and begins to transform our lives. In the midst of our failure, God wraps us in his love and assures us of his faithfulness, which makes us love him even more. Remember, he has already shown his love to the fullest extent:

> God demonstrates his own love for us in this: While we were still sinners, Christ died for us (Romans 5:8).

> This is love: not that we loved God, but that he loved us and sent his Son as an atoning sacrifice for our sins (1 John 4:10).

We will never genuinely know the love of God until we realize just what Christ accomplished for us through his death on the cross. Understand that you are totally forgiven, and his love will take on new meaning and power in your life. You will be able to say, just as the apostle Paul did,

> What, then, shall we say in response to these things? If God is for us, who can be against us? He who did not spare his

> own Son, but gave him up for us all—how will he not also, along with him, graciously give us all things? Who will bring any charge against those whom God has chosen? It is God who justifies. Who then is the one who condemns? No one. Christ Jesus, who died—more than that, who was raised to life—is at the right hand of God and is also interceding for us. Who shall separate us from the love of Christ? Shall trouble or hardship or persecution or famine or nakedness or danger or sword? As it is written: "For your sake we face death all day long; we are considered as sheep to be slaughtered." No, in all these things we are more than conquerors through him who loved us (Romans 8:31-37).

We all know that the world is not yet repaired—that evil, sin, and troubles abound on every side. Sometimes those troubles involve literal persecution for the people of God. But throughout the centuries, faithful Christians have found that they have "the peace of God, which transcends all understanding" (Philippians 4:7) through the love of Christ and the power of the Holy Spirit. So Paul can triumphantly conclude,

> I am convinced that neither death nor life, neither angels nor demons, neither the present nor the future, nor any powers, neither height nor depth, nor anything else in all creation, will be able to separate us from the love of God that is in Christ Jesus our Lord (Romans 8:38-39).

If you are a believer in Jesus Christ, this is your inheritance through the New Covenant. If in any way you are unsure, I urge you: Don't turn the page until you have finalized the cross in your life, and claimed all that is yours through him who loved us, and who loves us today and forever.

11

Rest for the Soul
The Relaxation of Knowing Christ

Come to me, all you who are weary and burdened, and I will give you rest. Take my yoke upon you and learn from me, for I am gentle and humble in heart, and you will find rest for your souls.
MATTHEW 11:28-29

Florida. It's my favorite vacation spot. I love the sand, the ocean breezes, the beautiful clear water, and the warm sun. To me, there is nothing more relaxing than a walk on the beach. Feeling the sand between my toes and the warm sun on my back clears my mind and refreshes my soul.

My mom and dad introduced me to Florida as a kid. Every summer our family made the trip from Indiana to the white sand beaches along the Gulf Coast. Of all the memories I have of my family, my fondest are of those of our times together in Florida. I have continued the tradition as an adult. I have visited many exciting places around the world, but my favorite spot is still Florida. Amy and I go there as often as we can.

Spiritually speaking, God has a destination for us that provides rest for the soul. This is not a place we visit occasionally. Once we arrive at this rest, we are to stay there permanently. Now our ultimate destination as children of God is heaven, and we look forward to that day when we will be in his presence forever. However, his purpose for us here and now is called the Sabbath rest.

Coming to God's Place of Rest

The writer of Hebrews compares this spiritual destination to the Promised Land. God did not lead the Israelites out of Egypt to wander in the desert. He had a specific destination in mind for them. This destination was a land flowing with milk and honey, complete with wells for drinking water and lush trees with every kind of fruit. Everything the people needed was already in place, and it was there for the taking. (Doesn't this remind you of 2 Peter 1:3—"His divine power has given us everything we need for a godly life"?)

All the Israelites had to do to enter this fabulous land was to trust God for the ability. The Lord promised to fight their battles for them. It was no more than an 11-day journey from Egypt if traveled from point A to point B, but we know the story. Instead of making an 11-day journey, the Israelites roamed the desert for 40 solid years. Why? *Because of their unbelief.* Despite the Lord's miraculous deliverance from their Egyptian slavery, despite the numerous miracles they had already seen, they did not trust the Lord for the steps ahead that would have taken them to their final destination.

Not many weeks after leaving Egypt, the Israelites arrived at the desert of Zin and stayed in a place called Kadesh. There was no water to be found. The people gathered to quarrel and grumble with Moses and Aaron: "Why did you bring the Lord's community into this wilderness, that we and our livestock should die here? Why did you bring us up out of Egypt to this terrible place? It has no grain or figs, grapevines or pomegranates. And there is no water to drink!" (Numbers 20:4-5).

In other words, they were saying that God might have had the power to pound the Egyptians into submission, deliver them—the Israelites—from the angel of death on the night of the Passover, part the Red Sea to provide a way of escape, and provide manna daily for their meals—but apparently he was unable to provide water for them to drink!

Isn't that just like you and me sometimes? Despite the Lord's work of salvation through Jesus Christ, despite our past experience with him where he has given us good gifts and provided for us up to the present…we still doubt him in our present situation. It's as if we're saying, "I know you have done all those things for me, Lord, but what have you done for me lately?" Sometimes we aren't so different from those ancient Israelites.

Forty years later, after the death of the unbelieving generation of Israelites, Joshua would lead the people of Israel into the Promised Land. As with their deliverance from Egypt, entering the Promised Land would require a supernatural work of God. Just as He parted the Red Sea, God parted the waters of the Jordan River, and the people crossed over on dry land. God did the work. The people entered by faith.

This tells us something very important about the Christian life today, as the writer of Hebrews makes clear in chapters 3 and 4 in his discussion of the "Sabbath rest." Just as we could do nothing to contribute to our salvation but to humbly receive by faith what Christ has done, neither can we contribute our own efforts to experiencing the fullness of life in Christ. We enter into Christ's fullness in the same way the Israelites entered the land: By faith in his finished work.

It was a new generation of Israelites who took possession of the land, a land where they would enjoy the provision of God, lean on the protection of God, and live in the power of God. This would be a whole new way of life for them. No longer would they have to suffer at the hands of slave masters. This new land was a land of freedom, a place where they could live out their identity as the free people of God.

Our Promised Land

God's destination for our spiritual journey is also waiting for us. All that is necessary is for us to enter and enjoy his Sabbath rest by faith.

Christ has accomplished everything on our behalf. He has prepared the way for us to experience total forgiveness and to stand before God the Father accepted and righteous in his sight. He has opened the way for us to enjoy a personal and intimate relationship with him. It is there for the taking if we choose to enter by faith. This is why the writer of Hebrews says,

> There remains, then, a Sabbath-rest for the people of God; for anyone who enters God's rest also rests from their works, just as God did from his (Hebrews 4:9-10).

He also gives us this warning:

> Therefore, since the promise of entering his rest still stands, let us be careful that none of you be found to have fallen short of it (4:1).

Yet the vast majority of Christians seem to have missed it, and they wander about in the spiritual desert of legalism, where their souls grow weary and tired. They live there because they either don't know about, or refuse to rest in, Christ's finished work. Remember, he did it *all*— there is nothing for us to do but live by faith, being led by the Holy Spirit.

Unbelief is what causes Christians to struggle to make sense of Christianity. Living in unbelief is not God's desire for you or for any of his children.

Where would you locate yourself in this story? Are you one who has taken firm hold of all the promises of God in the New Covenant, or would you describe yourself as living a "desert experience"? If it's the latter, you don't have to stay there. The Christian life does not have to be arid, fruitless drudgery. Christ's promise stands, and the Sabbath-rest life is available for the claiming.

To enjoy this promise, however, you must abandon trust in all your works that are done to earn, or merit, God's love and forgiveness. No matter how hard you try, no matter how sincere the effort you expend, your good works miss the target of his righteousness in every way. In his sight, our religious efforts are nothing more than filthy rags. The New Covenant is entirely based on faith. Therefore,

- *Quit trying to earn God's righteousness.* As Paul wrote emphatically, "No one will be declared righteous in God's sight by the works of the law" (Romans 3:20). But the good news is this: "God made him who had no sin to be sin for us, so that in him we might become the righteousness of God" (2 Corinthians 5:21). You stand righteous in God's sight by his love and mercy through Jesus Christ. It is impossible to add—there is no need to add—to the righteousness of Christ you have by faith in him!

- *Let go of all human traditions you relied on as important to your spirituality,* those you thought were marks of the Christian life. They may make you feel better about yourself or make you look more "spiritual" in the eyes of others, but if they are not based in biblical truth, they are nothing more than empty and deceptive philosophies. Paul warned about these in his letter to the Colossians: "See to it that no one takes you captive through hollow and deceptive philosophy, which depends on human tradition and the elemental spiritual forces of this world rather than on Christ" (Colossians 2:8).

- *Stop asking God for what you already have in Christ.* In Him, forgiveness is yours. You can ask, beg, and even bargain for more, but all your pleas will not make you any more forgiven: "In him *we have* redemption through his blood, *the forgiveness of sins,* in accordance with the riches of God's grace that he lavished on us" (Ephesians 1:7-8). Jesus shed his blood. All the work God required concerning your forgiveness has been done. If you are "in him" (which every believer is), you *possess* eternal forgiveness—now. There is nothing left for you to do. Believe it to be true, and rest in him!

How do you respond to this? It may be that this is the greatest news you have ever heard. It may be that you think it sounds too good to be true. It's also possible, if you have been strongly trained under legalistic teaching, that your religious sensibilities are revolting right now. But I assure you—resting from your works and placing the full weight of your trust in the work of Christ is the mark of the New Covenant believer who comprehends "this grace in which we now stand" (Romans 5:2).

This is your spiritual inheritance, your destination, your promised land. Read again these words from the writer of Hebrews:

> There remains, then, a Sabbath-rest for the people of God;
> for anyone who enters God's rest also rests from their works,
> just as God did from his (Hebrews 4:9-10).

If you haven't entered into God's rest, the promise still stands. Let today be your day. Rest from your work, just as God rested from his. Put down the burden of performance and enjoy the freedom and grace purchased for you by Jesus Christ.

The Sabbath for the New-Covenant Believer

You recall the creation story as recorded in Genesis. God created everything that was, including humanity, in six days. Each day, God looked at what he had created and saw that it was good. For each of those days we observe a pattern: "And there was evening, and there was morning." The seventh day, however, was different. On this day, God rested. His work was finished. Creation was complete. As Genesis 2:3 states, "God blessed the seventh day and made it holy, because on it he rested from all the work of creating that he had done."

Something else is noticeably different about this seventh day. The phrase, "and there was evening, and there was morning" is conspicuously absent. Why? The Bible doesn't answer specifically, but the open-endedness suggests an eternal quality regarding the Sabbath, that it is a rest to be experienced continually, every day and forever.

The Old Covenant relegated the Sabbath to the seventh day of the

week, what we know as Saturday. Based on the Genesis account of creation, evening, or sundown, was the beginning of a new day. Israel's
weekly honoring of the Sabbath began at sundown every Friday and
ended at sundown Saturday. Because the resurrection of Jesus occurred
on the first day of the week, many Christians believe that Sunday is
now the Sabbath. Hundreds of callers to the *People to People* radio
broadcast have asked me about this.

Speaking in terms of Moses' Law, the Sabbath is Saturday. That
has not changed. However, the fourth commandment, like everything
else in the Law, was merely a shadow. The command to Israel to keep
the Sabbath day holy foreshadowed a reality that could only be experienced through faith in Jesus Christ. Paul explained it this way:

> Let no one pass judgment on you in questions of food and
> drink, or with regard to a festival or a new moon or a Sab-
> bath. These are a shadow of the things to come, *but the
> substance belongs to Christ* (Colossians 2:16-17 ESV).

The *substance* of the fourth commandment is an eternal rest in the
finished work of Jesus Christ. Every day that we live, not just one day
a week, is a day to rejoice in all that he accomplished and to thank him
for his gift of grace in our lives. For the Christian, *every* day is a Sabbath day—a day to trust God and enjoy his rest!

Adam and Eve were the first to marvel at the work of God's hands.
Can you imagine what they felt as they looked upon all that he had
created? Joy, gladness, and thanksgiving in the purest and most sincere
form flowed from their hearts. Everything they needed to experience
life to the full was before them. There was nothing for them to add. Life
for Adam and Eve began in a state of rest, and all their life experience
was to flow from that rest.

We know the story. Sin entered in and robbed Adam and Eve
of their rest. No longer were they singing the praises of God's work.
Instead, they became absorbed with their own. They found out, however, that sewing together fig leaves didn't accomplish anything as far
as God was concerned. So they tried something else and then, when
that didn't work, they tried again. Since that time, people have been

offering up the works of their hands to God in hopes that he would be pleased. But those works never even approach being good enough, and the rest that was lost in the Garden is never achieved.

God, however, spoke of another day, a day the fourth command-ment of the Old Covenant foreshadowed. It is the day on which we enter into our promised land, the day we marvel at the work of Jesus Christ on our behalf. It is the day Jesus' death, burial, and resurrec-tion makes us glad and fills our hearts with thankfulness. I hope that through the chapters of this book, you have seen the work of Jesus Christ with fresh eyes and are now convinced that in Him you have everything you need for life and godliness. This is the message of the New Covenant. This is your destination. Have you entered in? If not, make today the day. There is new life to be enjoyed. Say thank you, rejoice in the work of Jesus, and take hold of this new life of faith in him that is yours in him.

The Guarantee

The promise of complete and final forgiveness of sins is the prom-ise that guarantees all the others of the New Covenant. It is also our entry point into New Covenant living. The blood of Jesus provides the confidence for us to enter in and share in our eternal inheritance. The writer of Hebrews speaks of this confidence:

> Since we have confidence to enter the Most Holy Place by the blood of Jesus, by a new and living way opened for us through the curtain, that is, his body, and since we have a great priest over the house of God, let us draw near to God with a sincere heart and with the full assurance that faith brings, having our hearts sprinkled to cleanse us from a guilty conscience and having our bodies washed with pure water. Let us hold unswervingly to the hope we profess, for he who promised is faithful. And let us consider how we may spur one another on toward love and good deeds (Hebrews 10:19-24).

The blood of Jesus provides the confidence we need to experience the entirety of the New Covenant. Wavering in belief concerning total forgiveness of sins puts the other three promises mentioned in this passage out of reach. How could we go boldly into the presence of God with a guilty conscience? How could we boldly assert that we possess assurance of salvation if the sin issue was still unresolved in our minds? How could we say that God's laws are written on our hearts and minds if we are still trying to clean up the sins of the flesh? For so many of us, trying to perfect ourselves—and we usually have our behavior in mind—is the sole focus of the Christian life. This is an impossible pursuit. Forgiveness is the key. It is the platform on which the New Covenant is built. So let's look back at the promises of the New Covenant in reverse order, and see what we can learn:

- *Total forgiveness of sins.* The promise of forgiveness through Christ's finished work on the cross enables us to rest in the acceptance of a holy God. This is not just "initial" forgiveness on the day we first believe, but a promise of forgiveness past, present, and future. We never again need to fear the punitive judgment of God because "there is now *no condemnation* for those who are in Christ Jesus" (Romans 8:1).

- *An intimate relationship with the Father.* Having been given a standing of complete acceptability, we are free to get to know our heavenly Father. He has provided a complete salvation for us so we can know him, and know his love in a life-changing way. What he wants in return, amazingly, is for us to love him. This giving and receiving of the love of God goes on to be the power center for Christian living. As Paul said, "Christ's love compels us" (2 Corinthians 5:14).

- *Unconditional acceptance.* Knowing that we are forgiven through Christ's finished work and knowing that we have a relationship with the Father, we can rest in his unconditional acceptance. We can know that our service and obedience can come freely from the love we offer back to him: "We love because he first loved us" (1 John 4:19).

- *A new heart.* The first three truths in themselves provide all the motivation we need in order to live on a new level, but that's not all God has done. The Lord promised to do a unilateral work within us, raising us to spiritual life in Christ and putting his own Spirit within us. We now have his laws of faith, hope, and love written on our hearts and in our minds. As we are led by his Spirit, he teaches us to do God's will and love others just as Christ loved us. As we trust, we discover that we aren't going *against* our own new natures—rather, we are acting *according to who we really are now*, beloved children of the living God. "You were once darkness, but now you are light in the Lord. Live as children of light" (Ephesians 5:8).

When you begin to grasp the totality of the New Covenant promises and their implications, you begin to see why we are told that we lack nothing we need to live genuine Christian lives. On the contrary,

> Praise be to the God and Father of our Lord Jesus Christ, who *has blessed us* in the heavenly realms *with every spiritual blessing in Christ* (Ephesians 1:3).

The Christian life is not "starting out with Jesus, and then looking for something better or more." It is starting with Christ and ending with Christ, the Alpha and Omega, the "I AM"—and then spending eternity discovering that in him we have everything we will ever need!

The main question, then, is how we begin to translate all these spiritual blessings we already possess into daily reality in thinking and behavior.

Life in the Land

Entering the Sabbath rest is just the beginning—the beginning of what God has in store for you. However, if you don't enter, the life God has for you will never be more than a distant blur on the horizon. I lived in the spiritual desert like many Christians do, and it almost destroyed me. That desert snatched away my joy and created a legalistic religionist. I did thrive for a period of time in the desert. Or I really should say that my legalistic pride provided a good report of it. The problem with the report was…it wasn't true. When I finally looked at my life, I was a mess. Joy and peace eluded me. Quite frankly, I had become a slave to my own fleshly desires and religious works.

I was working, almost panting, to keep myself forgiven. I was working to try to make myself holy. I was working to try to make myself more righteous in the sight of God. I was working to, hopefully, keep God loving me. I was working for the approval of others. I became a "menpleaser," as the King James Version puts it. Even with all my efforts on all these fronts, I never knew if I had done enough. This wasn't New Covenant living. The New Covenant promises assurance, freedom, and power, not the bondage I was experiencing. However, I had grown so accustomed to these religious activities that letting go was difficult. I had to switch tracks like a train.

But God's Spirit kept pressing the truth of my forgiveness in Christ, my righteous standing before God through faith in him, and the reality of Christ alive and living in me. He kept leading me to that point of rest and belief, to that place where I fully embraced the work of Jesus Christ as sufficient on my behalf. When I arrived, joy and peace flooded my inner being—and this was just the beginning. You have to enter the door that says, *It is finished!* to experience all that God has provided.

To Timothy, his young son in the faith, Paul offered this encouragement:

> Take hold of the eternal life to which you were called when you made your good confession in the presence of many witnesses (1 Timothy 6:12).

There is a life to be lived in the Promised Land, and that life is there for the taking once we rest in the finished work of Christ. As Paul urged, take hold of this life—Christ's life—and experience it to the full. But how?

The New Dynamic

The night before his death Jesus taught his disciples about the coming Holy Spirit and the new dynamic by which they would live. Jesus said,

> I am the vine; you are the branches. If you remain in me and I in you, you will bear much fruit; apart from me you can do nothing (John 15:5).

Think about a branch. Does a branch *produce* fruit or *bear* fruit? The distinction is critical. If you say a branch can "produce" fruit, you are saying it is the source of the result. But just cut a branch off an apple tree, for example, and watch how many apples it will produce. None! The branch is not the source of the life that produces the fruit. It is just a conduit, a means for the life, or the sap, of the tree to produce fruit. A branch is just a "fruit hanger"! It has no power, in and of itself, to produce a single bit of fruit.

But if that branch clings onto the true source, the trunk arising from the roots, and receives the life of the tree, allowing a free flow of sap, the result will be fruit. The branch will then *bear* fruit, the visible expression of the inner life.

Jesus is teaching us what the genuine Christian life is all about. The stunning truth is that *we cannot live it*. As he says, "Apart from me you can do *nothing*"! Now, by "nothing," he does not mean we cannot do activities. We can pile activity on top of activity in the name of Jesus, but that is not the same thing as fruit. What he means by fruit is the real thing, the genuine life of Christ, who lives in us, being expressed outwardly. That we cannot do by ourselves. Just as a branch can only *bear* fruit, you and I can only *bear* the Christian life. We cannot *produce* it.

Therefore, point one about genuine New Covenant living is to accept the fact that the Christian life is not *hard*—it is *impossible*. Only Christ can live it. So we have been given this marvelous promise:

> His divine power has given us everything we need for a godly life through our knowledge of him who called us by his own glory and goodness (2 Peter 1:3).

Did you notice that Peter said we have been given everything we need? We lack nothing in Christ. This sounds like God's description of the Promised Land. The people of Israel didn't have to dig wells for water or plant trees for food. Everything was provided for them. And so it is with us. We are complete in Christ, blessed with every spiritual blessing. Take hold of this life by abiding in him.

As you do, count on experiencing the fruit of the Spirit, which is "love, joy, peace, forbearance, kindness, goodness, faithfulness, gentleness and self-control. Against such things there is no law" (Galatians 5:22-23).

The Life of Freedom

Legalistic people fear freedom. They are afraid that if law isn't taught, people will go wild without standards. But they are apparently unfamiliar with the fact that Christ lives in the believer. If I'm not under the Law, why shouldn't I steal? Because the Christ who lives in me isn't a thief. If I'm not under the Law, why shouldn't I lie? Because the Christ who lives in me isn't a liar. As children of God, we are to be led by the Spirit. Learn to listen to him. We can trust that he will lead us into all truth and empower us to carry out his desires in this world.

We are free—free from the bondage and condemnation of the law, free from the power of sin, free from our fear of death. But even more importantly, we are free to live by faith in Jesus Christ and express his love one to another. Paul had this in mind when he wrote,

> You, my brothers and sisters, were called to be free. But do not use your freedom to indulge the flesh; rather, serve one another humbly in love. For the entire law is fulfilled in keeping this one command: "Love your neighbor as yourself" (Galatians 5:13-14).

New Covenant freedom means we have the privilege of pursuing the very best God has to offer. If anyone ever knew this, it was the man whose words we've considered throughout this book, the man who may have been the greatest legalist of all time:

> If someone else thinks they have reason to put confidence
> in the flesh, I have more: circumcised on the eighth day, of
> the people of Israel, of the tribe of Benjamin, a Hebrew
> of Hebrews; in regard to the law, a Pharisee; as for zeal,
> persecuting the church; as for righteousness based on the
> law, faultless (Philippians 3:4-6).

This is the apostle Paul speaking of his life as Saul of Tarsus, disciple of the great rabbi Gamaliel. There was no nation in history more religious than Israel. Benjamin was a royal tribe. There were no Jews more religious than the Pharisees, and Paul was one of the fastest-climbing stars within that system. His practice of the Law was so scrupulous, he says that according to that standard he was "faultless"—blameless.

Paul was closing in on the highest rung on the legalistic ladder. Shouldn't that have been enough? No. He found that his ladder had been leaning against the wrong wall. There was something far better:

> But whatever were to gains to me I now consider loss *for the sake of Christ*. What is more, I consider everything a loss *because of the surpassing worth of knowing Christ Jesus my Lord*, for whose sake I have lost all things. I consider them garbage, *that I may gain Christ* (Philippians 3:7-8).

Freedom to Know Christ

For me, all roads in the Bible lead here. I believe that God wants to lead every single one of his children to this place, where they recognize that nothing in this world compares to knowing Christ himself. What can religion add to him? How can legalism compare with him? What could you or I do to improve on him?

As a matter of fact, all of our efforts to earn acceptance based on keeping God's Law or human laws only get in the way of knowing him. That's why Paul goes on:

> …and be found in him, not having a righteousness of my own
> that comes from the law, but that which is through faith in
> Christ—the righteousness that comes from God on the basis
> of faith (verse 9).

The apostle realized that this was a fork in the road. He could continue to trust in his own legalistic righteousness based on keeping laws, or he could choose to humbly accept the true righteousness that God gives to anyone who puts their sole trust in Christ. One or the other—but you can't have both. And Christ can only be known where we put away confidence in ourselves and cast ourselves completely on him to be our forgiveness, righteousness, and life. Paul continues:

> *I want to know Christ*—yes, to know the power of his resurrection and participation in his sufferings, becoming like him in his death, and so, somehow, attaining to the resurrection from the dead.
>
> Not that I have already obtained all this, or have already arrived at my goal, *but I press on* to take hold of that for which Christ Jesus took hold of me (verses 10-12).

Paul had a privilege you and I have not enjoyed: He got to see the risen, glorified Christ. That vision utterly wiped away any confidence in the Law. By means of legalistic pursuits you can climb up a ladder people might admire, but you can't get to the glory possesssed by Christ. But having seen him, Paul wants everything Christ is and can give. The apostle knows he has not yet obtained everything God has for him and will not in this life, but notice—he *presses on*. That's what New Covenant transformation does to a person.

> Brothers and sisters, I do not consider myself yet to have taken hold of it. But one thing I do: Forgetting what lies behind and straining toward what is ahead, I press on toward the goal to win the prize for which God has called me heavenward in Christ Jesus (verses 13-14).

What does the New Covenant do when it fully grips a human heart and mind? It looks like this. It moves people to abandon everything behind—all self-trust, self-righteousness, and self-effort—and to become completely surrendered to and enamored with Jesus Christ. New Covenant truth only fires your heart to higher and greater fervor, with the desire to know him, experience his resurrected life, and to make yourself available to the leading of his Spirit, who shares in his life.

New Covenant understanding is what we were made for. It is truth that sets you free. It is love that compels you to serve willingly. It is a Person "in whom are hidden all the treasures of wisdom and knowledge" (Colossians 2:3).

New Covenant reality enables you to have Christ. And when you have Christ, you have God's *Everything*. You are rich beyond measure.

A Personal Invitation

December 30, 2009, started out as a typical day for me. It was a Wednesday. Amy and I ate breakfast at our favorite restaurant, and then I drove to the office for our noontime Bible study. I wasn't feeling well, but I wasn't that concerned. I called my son-in-law, who is a doctor, and asked if he could drop by the house after work to check me out. I told the radio team I would call into the ministry's studio from home and do the broadcast from there.

I made it home just fine. I connected to the studio without any problems. At 3:30 the program began. One particular caller asked a question concerning the purpose of the Law. It was a question I've answered hundreds of times, but that day I had the overwhelming sense I needed to teach on the New Covenant. For the next 20 minutes, I taught through the entirety of the New Covenant, pleading with our listeners to enter into God's rest—to rest from their works just as God had rested from his.

The program ended. An hour later, John, my son-in-law, arrived. He took my blood pressure and checked my temperature and pulse. Everything seemed normal. He was about to leave, but something stopped him. He came back into our family room to ask me another question. I tried to answer, but drew a blank. I couldn't speak. My eyes glazed over. John and Amy acted quickly. They put me into the car and rushed me to the nearest hospital. Tests confirmed John's suspicions. I had had a stroke.

The stroke had damaged the communication center of my brain. My ability to speak was gone. I could say a few words, but that was it. The hope was that over time, my speech would return and I could resume teaching my true passion and joy—the New Covenant. I went to speech therapy three days a week and did improve, but not a great deal. It has been over two years now, and I am still struggling. As you can imagine, this has been an extremely frustrating experience for me. I try to share what I know to be true, but the words will not come correctly.

I take comfort, though, in this. For the past 20 years, I have said time and time again that if I had only one message to give, it would be the message of the New Covenant. I had one last opportunity to do so, on December 30, 2009, when, as I told you, God moved in my heart to teach this life-changing message one last time. If I only had one message to give…

I am so pleased that this book is now in print. And I am very grateful to those who helped put it together. As I did on that last radio broadcast, I do here: I beg you to enter into the Sabbath rest, to take hold of your new life in Christ and the inheritance that is yours in him, and to live fully in the love and grace of God. Declare yourself to be a New Covenant believer. Your life will never be the same.

If you have received Jesus Christ through reading Jesus Changes Everything *or if your life has been impacted in other ways through the ministry of this book, you may find out more at my website, BobGeorge.net. May God bless you with a deep personal understanding and experience of his matchless love and grace!*

You may reach us at **bobandamygeorge@yahoo.com**. *You may also purchase my books and access many years of radio teaching programs at* **BobGeorge.net**.

About Bob George

At age 36, Bob George came to know Jesus Christ as Lord and Savior. Two years later he left his successful business to become involved in full-time ministry. With the emphasis on "full-time," he began to experience the heartache of losing his first love, Jesus Christ. Bob's resulting search for truth led him to the love and acceptance of God that was there all along.

Years of ministry, in both personal and group settings, fostered in Bob's heart a passion to communicate the love and grace of God to hurting people throughout the nation and the world. Thus, in 1977, Bob founded Dallas-based People to People Ministries.

For many years, he hosted *People to People*, a daily radio broadcast. Connecting with listeners across the continent on his live, daily radio broadcast, Bob offered real answers for real life as he addressed common questions as well as the tough issues of today, directing callers to the centrality of "Christ in you," your only hope of glory (Colossians 1:27).

Bob is the author of the bestselling book *Classic Christianity*, with an estimated 650,000 copies in print worldwide in 27 languages. Bob also has authored several other books, including *Growing in Grace, Victory over Depression, Complete in Christ,* and *Jesus Changes Everything,* as well as numerous Bible study guides.

Bob and his wife, Amy, author of *Goodbye Is Not Forever*, live in Dallas, Texas. They have two children and four grandchildren.

Also by Bob George

Classic Christianity

Life's Too Short to Miss the Real Thing

For every Christian who's deeply fulfilled, there are many more who are "doing all the right things" but still feel frantic or frustrated...or who've decided that Christianity's a failure. *What is it that's missing?*

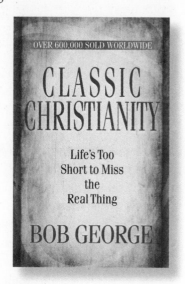

Like so many believers, Bob George began his Christian life in love with Jesus, only to end up feeling disappointed and empty. He draws on those struggles and his years of teaching and counseling experience and cuts straight to the heart of the issues that cause so many believers to start out excited—only to end up "going through the motions" or giving up entirely. The questions dealt with include...

- I know God loves me, but does he *accept* me?
- If I'm a new creation, why do I still struggle with sin?
- What does it mean to have Christ living *in* me?

In *Classic Christianity,* you'll see the way back to the life Jesus provided, a life set free from the bondage of the law, lived in the newness of his Spirit, and secure in his love.

Classic Christianity Study Guide

Life's Too Short to Miss the Real Thing

In the Christian life, a feeling of burnout or disappointment can often come from the attempt to live it in your own strength. How can you learn to rest in *God's* strength and find the freedom of his liberating love and grace? This study guide for *Classic Christianity* takes you deeper into every subject presented in the book. Scripture verses, questions, and relevant examples help you apply the Bible's truth and grasp who you are in Christ.

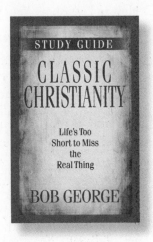

Growing in Grace

When Giving It All You've Got Still Isn't Enough

If your only experience of God's grace is being born again, you're missing half the good news. The other half is equally wonderful—Jesus wants you to experience his grace every day as he lives his life through you!

As a Christian, saved by grace and set free by grace, your next step is to grow in grace. As you mature, you'll be able to celebrate the truth of the Bible…giving up guilt and anxiety, letting go of legalism, and freshly discovering the joy of Jesus Christ living his life in and through you!

Includes helpful study guide for individual and small-group learning.

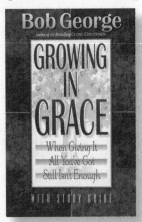

Victory over Depression

How to Live Above Your Circumstances

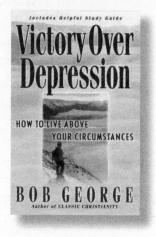

Depression. Hopelessness. Anger. Despondency. Sadness. These are some of the feelings you might experience when faced with difficult circumstances. But God has a bigger purpose for you than just getting rid of your problems. He wants you to *live above them.*

With a compassionate heart, Bob George shares how you can experience the reality of Jesus Christ as your hope in the midst of any seemingly hopeless situation. Whether poor relationships, past mistakes, personal tragedy, career or financial struggles, or illness, you can live above these circumstances by resting in the God who is far greater than any problem life can bring your way.

To learn more about Harvest House books and
to read sample chapters, log on to our website:

www.harvesthousepublishers.com

HARVEST HOUSE PUBLISHERS
EUGENE, OREGON